Highlights on Reinsurance History

P.I.E. Peter Lang
Bruxelles · Bern · Berlin · Frankfurt am Main · New York · Oxford · Wien

André Straus and Leonardo Caruana de las Cagigas (eds.)

Highlights on Reinsurance History

International Issues
Vol. 42

The book was subject to a double blind refereeing process.

Éditions scientifiques internationales
Bruxelles, 2017
1 avenue Maurice, B-1050 Bruxelles, Belgique
www.peterlang.com; brussels@peterlang.com

Printed in Germany

ISSN 2030-3688
ISBN 978-2-8076-0288-5
ePDF 978-2-8076-0289-2
ePub 978-2-8076-0290-8
Mobi 978-2-8076-0291-5
DOI 10.3726/b12250
D/2016/5678/31

Bibliographic information published by "Die Deutsche Nationalbibliothek".

"Die Deutsche Nationalbibliothek" lists this publication in the "Deutsche National-bibliografie"; detailed bibliographic data is available on the Internet at http://dnb.de.
Library of Congress Cataloging-in-Publication Data

Names: Straus, Andre, editor. | Caruana, Leonardo, editor. Title: Highlights on reinsurance history / Andre Straus and Leonardo Caruana, editors. Description: New York : Peter Lang, [2017] | Series: International issues ; Vol. 42 | Includes bibliographical references and index. Identifiers: LCCN 2017001488 (print) | LCCN 2017025641 (ebook) | ISBN 9782807602892 (E-book) | ISBN 9782807602908 (E-Pub) | ISBN 9782807602915 (Mobi) | ISBN 9782807602885 (alk. paper) Subjects: LCSH: Reinsurance-History. Classification: LCC HG8083 (ebook) | LCC HG8083 .H54 2017 (print) | DDC 368/.012209-dc23

LC record available at https://lccn.loc.gov/2017001488

Table of Contents

Introduction

Diversity in the Setting up of Reinsurance

Reinsurance specifically differs from insurance in that the insurance market is related to the clients (mainly people, companies, etc.) and reinsurance is related to insurance companies or reinsurance companies with an essential need of financial capability. In addition, reinsurance helps to develop the insurance market in underdeveloped countries and its headquarters are normally located at the geographical hub of the financial market in those countries.

From the Origins of Reinsurance to the Founding of Munich Re in 1880

Reinsurance has its own path of development; reinsurance companies evolved particular methods and expertise, although the origins of these are still debated by scholars.

It is well known, however, that the insurance industry gave birth to reinsurance. It began as a network of risk cover by several companies. These firms assumed part of the risk of other firms, then ceded to other companies part of that risk. A first company ceded to a second company, which also ceded to the first, and so on. The overall purpose – to diminish the risk – is known as coinsurance.

In the early days of reinsurance the problem was that the financial resources of the capital of a region or a country were insufficient to guarantee the risk. As a result, reinsurance became internationalized, with the fundamental characteristic that the reinsurance network is established through several countries.

In the 19th century reinsurance increased in importance. That does not mean that it began in the 19th century, because its origins clearly date from much earlier. We know that at the end of the 14th century in Genoa contracts of reinsurance already existed. However, its real development followed later and, as with many other changes in the insurance industry, came about through the requirements of maritime insurance, for which London was the geographical international center.

Clearly, the risks involved in sea voyages could be prolonged over several months and the insurance premiums for vessels were divided into several part-payments. A French treatise on maritime law, *Le Guidon de la Mer*, states: “If the insurers are afraid or repenting of signing a policy. It will be in their freedom to be reinsured by either a greater or lesser price.”

In France reinsurance developed independently (see the maritime regulation for 1681, which is included in the Code of Commerce, article 342). We do not have statistics for this period and it seems that the act of reinsurance was considered by some as if it was a game; worse, increasing speculation in this area obliged the English authorities to prohibit maritime reinsurance by a law of 1746. Some historians claim that it was intended only to prevent double insurance, but the phrasing of the law seems to make it clear that it did indeed refer to reinsurance. The prohibition was long-lasting, since the law was not repealed until 1867. The legislation prevented the normal development of the reinsurance market and increased coinsurance, especially through Lloyd’s of London, which grew rapidly as a reinsurer of large risk between subscribers.

In the first decades of the 19th century the reinsurance market developed further, thanks to contracts with fixed premiums that demanded beneficial results. The number of reinsurance contracts grew at the same time, far outstripping the numbers of coinsurance contracts. Another driver for change was the necessity of developing durable relationships with reinsurers. In fact the reinsurance operation was implemented immediately on the signing of an insurance policy, or in the reinsurance contract.

The first examples come from the field of fire insurance at the beginning of the 19th century, an area which was developing with the rule of reciprocity between insurance companies. In the case of reinsurance, the way in which the reinsurers saw “reciprocity” meant that the insurance companies also had to assume the same maximum put to reinsurers. This was done to increase transparency in setting premiums and assessing the risk. The reinsurers went into attack mode and demanded access to the embellished financial figures of the insurance companies. This, however, is exactly what the farsighted direct insurance companies had planned to avoid, in forming independent reinsurance companies. Almost immediately after the principle of “reciprocity” began to be used to define responsibilities, it was revised.

If we look for the first instance of accident insurance with reinsurance, we find it in 1888. The second half of the 19th century saw the attainment of greater autonomy by the reinsurance business. Foreign direct companies developing reinsurance became more dominant, owing to the different nature of their risk portfolio, which encouraged them to compete using information obtained by cedants; to avoid this, companies began to do business with a foreign company.

Soon, however, insurers thought to resist the disappearance of a portion of their profits with their assignment to others of their reinsurance and began to create their own reinsurance companies, totally in the control of their insurance company. This happened particularly in Germany in the course of 1840, when the impact of the fire of Hamburg reinforced the law of 1837, which made it compulsory for foreign companies to have an authorization to develop business in the country. The end result was the creation of the first pure reinsurance company: Cologne Reinsurance. The new company was the first of many in Germany: the Frankfurt in 1856, the Magdeburg in 1862, the Rheinische, and so on. In Switzerland the Swiss Company of Reinsurance started in 1863 and the same trend was noticeable in Austria-Hungary and Belgium. The foundation of these reinsurance companies had not only a great impact on the insurance companies themselves, but also on banks and financial institutions.

During the first wave of creation, companies were sometimes set up too hastily and in too great a number, especially in England; this generated fierce competition that often brought about the rapid disappearance of the new companies. Germany experienced the same 'reinsurance fever', but the companies were more robust, allowing Germany to occupy the first place worldwide in reinsurance.

From the Creation of the Munich Re to the First World War

Karl von Thieme (1844–1924) started the Münchener RückversicherungsGesellschaft, or Munich Re, in 1880. Thieme was born March 30, 1844 in Erfurt and died in 1924. Thieme began his association with the insurance business early in his working life and went to Munich as general agent for the Thuringia, where he soon demonstrated his gift for organization. Towards the end of the 1970s Thieme was asked to found a fire insurance company. The narrowness of the scope of the Thuringia operations led him to the idea of providing real insurance facilities for fire insurance. In addition, he felt that reinsurance could best be conducted as an independent and self-sufficient branch of the business. He secured a volume of business from the original insurers, on terms which would permit an independent company to survive, by holding a significant portion in direct companies.

Thieme's internationalism aimed to smooth out the effects of local fluctuations in business, climatic and operating conditions. Losses in one branch of the business in one country could be counterbalanced by gains in another branch in the same country. Alternatively, losses on all lines in one country would be compensated by gains in another country. The internationalization of reinsurance pioneered the widespread distribution of risk. Just before the First World War Munich Re was the largest single reinsurance company in the world[1].

The company had been born at the center of the insurance market and was very familiar with the sector dealing in fire, the principal sector for reinsurance. Thieme provided the principles that guided the development of the new company, which performed well in all sectors, but particularly in the newest. He was a great defender of the internationalization of reinsurance and of the importance of balancing financial participation between direct companies in Germany and companies abroad. The development of Munich Re heralded the beginnings of a unique German expertise in the industry. Almost simultaneously came its rapid spread to countries abroad, where this specialized skill set prevailed. The overriding success lay not with insurers creating subsidiary reinsurance companies, but with reinsurance which created direct insurance companies.

This German success only underlines more emphatically the failure of the English reinsurance companies. These companies were the victims of direct companies that did not support reinsurance companies, as was the case in Germany. Their failures were to the benefit of an inflated transport sector whose results were mediocre. Additional factors contributing to failure were strong reciprocal links between direct companies and a tardy understanding of the need to turn the business towards the international market, the real future theatre for reinsurance. This overall poor performance of the English reinsurance companies would be fatal. All except three would disappear between 1914 and 1922, thus obliging English dependency on "continental" companies in Germany or France, considered the homelands of reinsurance.

A survey of 1898 shows Germany in the leading position internationally, holding 37 domestic companies and over 67 companies across the globe. On the eve of the war, German had 44 companies with revenues that had doubled in ten years (end of 1915). In Europe at this time there were 143 reinsurance companies; of this total, 58 companies were German and had 47.3% of the total in premiums. Their business was spread around the world and especially over the American continent; the 20 million marks paid by the Munich Re when the fire destroyed San Francisco

---

1 Edwin W. Kopf (1929), *Notes on the Origin and Development of Reinsurance*, New York City, Globe Printing Company.

in 1907 are a good example of the extent of German dominance in the industry.

More than half of the productivity of these German firms lay in the area of fire reinsurance and only 5% in life insurance. Their exceptional development can perhaps be explained by the increase and importance of the financial reserves of the Munich Re, which rose from 415,000 marks in 1880–1881, to 3.78 million marks in 1890–1891, to more than 50 million marks in 1900–1901, and to practically 55 million in 1910–1911.

In any case, the most surprising achievement of the Germans in reinsurance was the premium income from foreign business of nearly 300 million marks against 550 million for sales of domestic firms. This success is, to a great extent, related to the early knowledge of the special characteristics of the reinsurance industry. As it is an international business, the strategy developed by firms was to conquer the world market, not only the German market. The goal was to become members on the administrative boards of a range of insurance companies and to achieve long-term collaboration with the ceding or new companies created by them as they struggled to penetrate existing markets.

The continental reinsurance business at the end of the 19th century was dominated by the force or capability of the German companies, but they were not alone. The Swiss success was essentially that of one firm, the Swiss Company of Reinsurance and its subsidiary company of Prudentia, created in 1875 on Austro-Hungarian territory.

We have seen that in Germany reinsurance was a powerful industry, with highly professional companies and a strong inclination by direct insurance companies to accept indirect affairs. At the end of the century fire insurance began to demand reinsurance in the Austro-Hungarian market. This localized growth of a specific market gave German companies a privileged position. German companies, and especially the Munich, came to have members on the boards of administration of several Austro-Hungarian companies, thus reinforcing their stake in the market; it is worth mentioning that access to this market had been lost by British companies, although they had been present in central Europe up to turn of the century. On the eve of the war German companies closely controlled the Austro-Hungarian market, using it to extend their business over the whole of the Danube region up to the Black Sea, the Balkans and into Italy. As far as Austria-Hungary was a cedant, Germany was pushing the Austro-Hungarian companies to expand eastward or even overseas. The control by German reinsurance of the Austro-Hungarian market therefore is not contradictory, but in keeping with Germany's leading role as reinsurance provider for Europe in 1914.

The international character of the reinsurance industry is again evident in the efforts of the Russian government at the end of the 19th century. The economic policy of Prime Minister Serguéi Witte was to develop a strong home-grown reinsurance business with the aim of avoiding the hegemony of foreign companies, because that would mean a loss in the balance of payments. Under his leadership two companies were added to the existing Russian companies: in 1893 the Society for Russian Reinsurance and, in 1895, the National Russian. Initially the outcome was disappointing, but by 1914 Witte's vision was successful, especially in fire insurance, and the results are largely a credit to reinsurance. Russia developed virtually no direct insurance abroad.

Reinsurance in Russia (nine companies in 1917) was a major player in northern Europe and in the United States. The three major providers of reinsurance in the world by 1914 were Germany, the Austro-Hungarian Empire and Russia. Now we will look at the dislocation that the war created.

From One War to the Next

The reinsurance industry had developed not only in Germany, Austria-Hungary and Russia, but was already in existence in Switzerland and Scandinavia. Belgium and France saw their markets developed by some companies dealing purely in reinsurance, but mainly by direct companies.

To a great extent World War I modified the reinsurance industry in Europe. The central empires lost the market of the allies, although for some periods of the war the ordinary business of reinsurance was maintained between enemies and, in specific cases, continued throughout the war.

Germany and Austria-Hungary had to concentrate their activity on their own markets, losing the international market where they had conducted a large part of their business, especially the American market. This loss, coupled with the collapse of the industry in Russia, benefited other countries and generated a new distribution of the international reinsurance market.

Some countries, such as Switzerland or Denmark, increased their activity to replace the vacuum left by the traditional leaders in reinsurance. Other countries would benefit from the new post-war boundaries, as was the case for Italy with the annexation of the city of Trieste at the dissolution of Austria-Hungary, and the newly created Czechoslovakia with Prague as its capital city. These two cities were main centers for fast-growing reinsurance companies; the first is well known for the famous company name Generali.

The end of the war was a fine moment to develop the reinsurance industry in several countries without the strong presence of the traditional market leaders, Germany, Russia and the dissolved Austro-Hungarian Empire, now divided into smaller countries. France provides a good example of the assertive development of national companies in the midst of this new European market.

Clearly, for the German reinsurance business, the greatest consequence of the war was the loss of the American market, especially in fire reinsurance. Far worse, however, was the hyperinflation in the first years of the 1920s, an inflation that was "solved" by a large number of cessions and saw many new companies quickly bankrupted. The concentration of effort begun back in 1880 benefited the best qualified companies, while the insurance sectors that suffered the greatest shock during the crisis were fire insurance and transport insurance.

The capacity for recovery lasted up to 1929. The Munich Re considered that the company was capable of recovering the position that it had had before the war, and the German reinsurance companies did in fact manage to regain the international market. But they had lost their pre-war solvency; in the American market the important clients that had been lost in the fire insurance sector were replaced by reinsurance in transport, a much riskier market after the First World War and one that had been abandoned by British brokers for that reason. The branches of accident reinsurance and other, less relevant, sectors such as credit were also developed after the war.

This changed landscape for the assurance and reinsurance industry could be observed globally. The changes may be largely explained by the appearance of new countries competing in the reinsurance industry and the shaky development of the reinsurance market after the war.

One of the best examples of this radically altered post-war situation can be seen in the new countries that came out of the dissolution of the Austro-Hungarian Empire. For example, the company Erste Bohmische Rückversicherungsbank became part of Czechoslovakia, because the headquarters of the company were in the city of Prague. Several other important companies survived the collapse of empire: in Austria the Wiener Rück continued, while in Hungary two companies, the Budapest and the Panonia, carried on their operations in the capital of the new country. With the Italian gain of Trieste, the Riunione Adriatica and the Assicurazioni Generali companies passed to Italian control because the headquarters of both were in this city. Moreover, they would take the place of German reinsurance companies in the market of Austria and in the European Danube region, also competing with the French and Swiss reinsurance companies in Rumania and Yugoslavia. In addition, Danish companies were new players in the Austrian and Hungarian markets. In the sector of fire reinsurance, the high qualifications of Austrian and Hungarian experts held their own in the national market. However, these companies were to disappear from the international reinsurance scene.

From 1945 to Today

During the Second World War, due to the rarefaction of supply in the market of professional reassurance, many insurers embarked on indirect business. This development has accelerated globally since 1950. Additionally, to meet the growing needs of the economy, direct insurers created their own reinsurance companies. Thus, conditions of fierce competition were produced, bringing with them changes of scale and structure in the reinsurance industry. There were five radical changes: more capacity; a shift from focus on technical results to financial performance[2]; a chronic tendency to offer insufficient tariffs; the appearance of captive companies to take part of the market; and finally, the foundation of new state companies, particularly in underdeveloped countries, increased supply.

Shortly after the Second World War, following the various shocks undergone since the late 1920s (the crisis of 1929, which hit reinsurance harder than direct insurance; the social crisis; the autarky response; and finally the Second World War itself), the international reinsurance market seems stabilized.

The German market, so important to the reinsurance industry on the eve of the war, only continued to develop due to the professionalism built up in this sector over decades and the extreme concentration of the market. In 1936 the Allianz-Münchener group controlled two thirds of the premiums, the Aachen-Münchener group one fourth of the premiums, followed by the Magdeburger-Gruppe and the Gerling-Konzern. The excess of acceptation in comparison with cession was significant, but far less so when compared with the statistics for the period before the First World War. Two elements can account for this weakening. Firstly, the reduction of the role played in the international market by German companies. Secondly, the change of method in the German reinsurance industry, with the development of business by subsidiary companies, as for example in America or in Switzerland. Finally, after the Second World War, the market

2 Technical result: Company result before return on investment, other income, costs and taxes.

was restricted to the territory of West Germany (American, British, French control) and any acceptance abroad was made impossible. Fortunately, this prohibition would disappear in 1950.

The Swiss

After the war Switzerland was one of the greatest exporters. The main characteristic of the market was the superiority of professional companies compared to mixed companies; this may be explained by the existence of the Swiss Reinsurance Company and its subsidiary the European as established market players. Even more significant, this company operated in close relationship with British, German, French and American companies. These were all professional reinsurance firms and, in addition, were the most important in their own countries. Moreover, the European Company held a significant proportion of shares in many direct insurance companies. With other European companies, the Swiss firms were the most important reinsurance companies in the world and Swiss and German expertise in professional reinsurance had no equivalent elsewhere.

The United States

In North America the insurance market functioned under inflationary conditions during and after the war. Nevertheless, there was a large requirement for an increase in reinsurance means. The few foreign reinsurance companies legally admitted to the US market notably suffered from a shortage of dollar reserves. Moreover, only a foreign country with a strong currency at home was able to meet local needs. This explains the important role played by Swiss companies in this market (Swiss Company and Swiss General Assurance), because the Swiss franc was strong. They developed reinsurance in the American market under their own names, or through their subsidiary companies. The French, British and Scandinavian companies also had a significant presence in the American market. The magnitude of the cession of American companies to the London market, especially through Lloyd's, was particularly remarkable. In contrast, US companies had not developed their acceptances in Europe to the level of their economic influence. Like many other branches of industry, US reinsurance was merely developed or concentrated in the domestic market. They feared European regulations because they could be asked to deliver reciprocity. Eventually the American reinsurance companies started to go abroad, mainly to Latin America and the Pacific region.

Great Britain

At the start of the war the development of the London market presented a strange scenario. We cannot forget that reinsurance was banned in 1746; consequently coinsurance developed massively, but this was not an impediment to London concentrating some of the most significant risks from around the world. The ban was lifted in 1864 and from 1870 onwards the first reinsurance brokers appeared, mainly to meet the growing need for reinsurance by British fire insurers[3]. After the First World War the main players in reinsurance, Germany and Switzerland, continued to consider London the hub of the reinsurance market[4].

In fact, only a small part of this business was British professional reinsurance. The City had a scant four companies dealing purely in reinsurance, the first of which dated from 1867 (Re-Insurance Co. Ltd). Nevertheless, Great Britain was by far the main center for maritime reinsurance in the world. Of note in this context was the pivotal role played by brokers in the business of reinsurance, a role as important in Britain as it was in the United States.

In most insurance markets the role of intermediaries, agents or brokers is usually important. Their remit is to scan the market and match clients, either the insured or primary insurers, with insurers or reinsurers. In the last case "Reinsurance brokers play an important intermediation role between primary (retail) insurers and reinsurers"[5]. But the physical presence of foreign reinsurance companies on the English market was rare. The conclusion could be drawn that this is not a typical reinsurance market, but rather a market whose conditions are very different from the others on the world scene.

Nordic Countries

The importance of reinsurance in these countries before the war continued after the Second World War. Two Scandinavian countries, Sweden and Denmark, were exporting reinsurance. Just before the war the Danish companies specialized, as did the Germans or Swiss, in life reinsurance (an

---

3 Peter Borscheid and Niels Viggo Haueter (eds) (2012), *World Insurance*, Oxford, Oxford University Press, p. 68.

4 Harold James, Peter Borscheid, David Gugerli and Tobias Strauman (2013), *The Value of Risk*, Oxford, Oxford University Press, p. 78.

5 J. David Cummins and Neil A. Doherty (2006), *The Journal of Risk and Insurance*, 73/3, p. 361.

outstanding example being the firm Dana). In Sweden's case, Aequitas, founded in 1944 by six companies, had more than double the market of the professional group. As with Denmark, they specialized in accepting life reinsurance. Significant new companies developing at this time were Sverige, with its chief focus on reinsurance premiums of risk[6], and Vala, a subsidiary of Aequitas. In the end the Danish reinsurance industry would become more significant on the international market than that of the Norwegians or the Swedes.

France

The French reinsurance business had developed expertise in the domestic market. The war did cut off a lot of the foreign business in the country, obliging direct exchanges between companies, with the result that businesses specializing purely in reinsurance expanded. Cooperative organisms played an important role and the nationalization of the biggest insurance companies provided a significant market for reinsurance. The state-controlled Caisse Centrale de Réassurance, founded in 1946, held a fixed percentage of private business and occupied an important place in the national and international markets.

The main cooperative groups of reinsurance after the war were Groupement de Réassurance Maritime and the Section de Réassurance Mutuelle. The market for professional reinsurance was still active. Net entries from professional societies stagnated in the 1930s, but the progression or performance of the business continued nonetheless. In 1945 accepted reinsurance by all French companies, including the Group of Algiers but excluding Agricultural Mutuality, amounted to 5.6 billion francs, from which 40% were retroceded. Of that amount, professional insurers accounted for half of the total, 2.85 billion, and they retroceded 38%; the difference between these two percentages is explained primarily by the policy of the Nord Africaine, which retroceded only 37 million francs of 683 million conceded.

Apart from this company, the French professional reinsurers retroceded significantly as mixed companies, which can be explained by the necessity to spread risks. Risk-spreading was essential because the importance of French business decreased in the accepted portfolio, thus reducing financial power against the backdrop of a devalued franc, and there also existed an obligation to provide reciprocally accepted booked premiums,

6 In reinsurance on a risk-premium basis, only a proportionate share in the capital at risk is reinsured. In term life insurance, the capital at risk is the same as the sum insured.

unlike mixed companies which took these booked premiums directly into their portfolio.

The French market had several characteristics: poor cession on motor insurance, civil responsibility and accidents at work. Reinsurance was strong in the areas where the risk is directly proportional to the amount insured, or the risk is significantly different (fire, robbery, and especially transport or catastrophe). Naturally, transport reinsurance was linked to, or heavily dependent on, Lloyd's of London, thus contributing to weighing down the balance of the sector. That there was less practice of reinsurance by the mutual than the stock companies can be explained in the first place by the lower risk, secondly by the lack of mutual maritime insurance, and finally by the fact that they functioned in pure mutuality (mortality and hail). The situation of the companies was dominated by the existence of an exceptionally well-placed French professional group that controlled half of the reinsurance accepted.

The major modifications to the reinsurance industry after the Second World War were institutional and technical. In the French administrative landscape constructed by Colbert the central government plays a major role and the post-war market saw the creation of state institutions for insurance, completed with the founding of the Nord Africaine. This would be damaging to German reinsurance, because France had been a traditional market. Additionally, other countries such as Argentina, Brazil, Chile, Turkey, Egypt and several African countries would create state monopolies. This had the effect of restricting the scope of activity for other reinsurers, often leading to the diminution of their business relationships with older institutes that had become monopolies.

However, the history of assurance companies involved in reinsurance is long, even older than business based purely on reinsurance itself. And insurance companies with heavy involvement in reinsurance played a major role during this period, since the war had curtailed or broken the international reinsurance network. The most positive results were seen in the sectors of fire and transport, which developed reinsurance in autonomous branches.

New forms of reinsurance were crafted. In addition to proportional reinsurance, reinsurance of excess loss appeared. Eventually the effort of the reinsurance industry to balance the portfolio between the different sectors was not satisfactory, largely due to the rapid development of motor industry sector. This lead to hard competition between insurers for a stake in the market, and the same competition generated lower prime rates. Consequently, the companies were weakened and forced to seek more and more motor reinsurance contracts.

Japan and the Far East[7]

The end of 19th century saw the emergence of the Japanese market and the reinsurance business was developed through foreign companies such as China Traders, Yangtze and Canton Insurance. The main player, Tokyo Marine Insurance Company, entered into tough competition with marine companies and shipping agents; after the company of Nihon Kairuku was forced into dissolution, the Tokyo Marine adopted the policy of reinsuring only by cession to London.

In India during the course of the 19th century occasional facultative reinsurance was developed by European companies and at the end of the century this was the norm.

Concept and Features of Reinsurance

Bouvier (1856) provided this definition: "Insurance made by a former insurer, his executors, administrators, or assigns, to protect himself and his estate from a risk to which they were liable by the first insurance"[8]. Historically reinsurance started with insurance companies[9], mainly because reinsurance is crucial to increase capital and earnings and reduce costs for the insurance companies[10].

Pruitt points out four aims of reinsurance: 1) to smooth out the peaks and valleys of experience; 2) to protect against the shock and loss of catastrophe; 3) to provide surplus relief, where over-expansion is a danger; and 4) to cut down the size of a line to digestible proportions[11]. In other words, financing, stabilization, capacity, and protection against catastrophe[12] are the key desirable outcomes. Following Johnson, in the process of growth an insurance company will need to reinsure for management purposes (financing). The loss ratios will stabilize through reinsurance over time, because profits can compensate for losses. Thanks to economies of scale,

---

7 Peter Borscheid and Niels Viggo Haueter (eds) (2012), *World Insurance*, Oxford, Oxford University Press, pp. 424 & 502.

8 http://www.constitutions.org.Bouvier.txt.

9 Matthew Rodermund (1965), "Four Points of Confusion about Reinsurance: Comment", *The Journal of Risk and Insurance*, 32/1, pp. 133–6.

10 Ron Adiel (1996), "Reinsurance and the Management of Regulatory Ratios and Taxes in the Property-Casualty Insurance Industry", *Journal of Accounting and Economics*, 22, pp. 207–40.

11 Dudley M. Pruitt (1958), "The Seat of Wisdom", *Proceedings of the Casualty Actuarial Society*, XLV, p. 16.

12 Munich Reinsurance Company (1963), *Reinsurance, What It Can Do For You.*

bigger reinsurance companies can take more risks. In the 1970s "the premium for the reinsurance … was broken down in successive $1 million layers of $2,000, $1,500, $1,000, $500, and $250"[13]. Finally, catastrophe protection is less predictable and is costly, so that repayments are much longer and companies usually reinsure this type of risk far more[14].

Insurance and reinsurance are relevant to economic growth, since private insurance is an important element of GDP. In the developed countries, insurance accounts for over 5% of GDP and generates employment and assets. The significance of this was mentioned at the United Nations Conference on Trade and Development in 1964[15] (UNCTAD 1964: 55). Insurance "promotes financial stability and reduces anxiety; can substitute for government security programs; facilitates trade and commerce; mobilizes savings; enables risk to be managed more efficiently; encourages loss mitigation; fosters a more efficient capital allocation"[16].

There are three approaches to reinsurance suggested by Modigliani and Miller: "The finance specialist is concerned with the techniques of financing firms so as to ensure their survival and growth"; "the managerial economist is concerned with capital budgeting"; and "the economic theorist is concerned with explaining investment behavior at both the micro and macro levels"[17]. The capital structure literature has suggested that firms actually have a target debt ratio, which is influenced by several factors such as size and profitability[18]. Shiu remarks: "insurers purchasing more reinsurance would have higher leverage, possibly because reinsurance purchases, like renting capital from reinsurers, increase the insurer's surplus, allowing the insurer to write more new policies, thereby increasing their leverage but maintaining a certain level of solvency"[19]. Rossi and Lowe remark that many countries indirectly regulate foreign reinsurers by: (1) restricting the amount of coverage domestic insurers can purchase from foreign reinsurers, or the particular reinsurers domestic

---

13 Richard E. Johnson (1977), "Reinsurance: Theory, the New Applications, and the Future", *The Journal of Risk and Insurance*, 44/1, p. 60.

14 *Ibid.*, pp. 55-66.

15 United Nations (1964), *Proceedings of the United Nations Conference on Trade and Development*: First Session, 1, Final Act and Report, Geneva, United Nations, p. 55.

16 Harold D. Skipper Jr. (1997), "Foreign Insurers in Emerging Markets: Issues and concerns", *IIF Occasional paper* 1, Washington, International Insurance Foundation, p. 11.

17 Franco Modigliani and Merton Miller (1958), "The Cost of Capital, Corporation Finance and the Theory of Investment", *The American Economic Review*, 48/3, pp. 261–97.

18 Sheridan Titman and Roberto Wessels (1988), "The Determinants of Capital Structure Choice", *The Journal of Finance*, 43/1, pp. 1–19.

19 Yung-Ming Shiu (2011), "Reinsurance and Capital Structure: Evidence from the United Kingdom Non-Life Insurance Industry", *The Journal of Risk and Insurance*, 78/2.

insurers can use; (2) requiring capital be held in national funds as a safety net; and/or (3) requiring large amounts of information concerning the reinsurers[20]. In addition, during the 1960s the IAIS (International Association of Insurance Supervisors), with 97% of the world's insurance premiums, developed international regulatory standards for reinsurers.

The reinsurance industry develops when insurance companies grow substantially and they need to reduce risk, so that they demand reinsurance premiums. This development has a second stage that leads them to open branches abroad, bringing further need to reduce risk and the demand for further reinsurance. This progression leads the reinsurance company to become international and, even if it is not the only route by which it becomes international, it is an important path for many reinsurance companies.

The insurance companies aim to develop business in more and more countries with two goals: profit maximization and to spread risk distribution. They all underwrite a large number of businesses, protecting them particularly from a single large loss (e.g., a major catastrophe). In furthering both goals reinsurance is necessary, because the companies cannot assume much risk. Therefore they transfer a percentage of the risk. In addition, as some countries impose restrictions on foreign insurance companies in the home market, or even drive them out, this indirectly increases the importance of the reinsurance business, for example during Franco's time in Spain. The same holds for countries where the insurance sector is nationalized. Yet dependence on foreign reinsurance is not eliminated, particularly in less developed countries, because the premium income is not high and reinsurance companies assume a high level of risk to balance their portfolios. Moreover, the growing size and complexity of risk in all sectors makes reinsurance necessary. The size of some countries and the size of the insurance market increases the importance of reinsurance, particularly in highly specialized risk, so that expertise from abroad is required.

To sum up, reinsurance is a global business because it can manage more risk and in more countries. However, companies can increase the level of risk in a country or a specific region. In fact, there should be a balance between local and global risk. Often many companies in one country prefer to reinsure abroad in order that the local companies do not know about the performance of their companies. Additionally, each company prefers the technical capability, good planning, experience and robust financial standing of a more advanced country such as Switzerland or Germany, which are orthodox financial markets with clear regulations and market discipline.

Although reinsurance is very important for insurance companies, it has received little scholarly attention. Those who have focused on it include Cecil

---

20 Marie-Louise Rossi and Nicholas Lowe (2002), "Regulating Reinsurance in the Global Market", *The Geneva Papers on Risk and Insurance*, 27, pp. 122–33.

Edward Golding and Edwin W. Kopf (in the 1920s), and (more recently) Robin Pearson, Harold James, Peter Borcheid and Niels V. Haueter, David Gugerli and Tobias Strauman[21].

World Reinsurance in the Last Decades

Great changes have taken place in the reinsurance sector, in spite of its need to sustain great stability. It has been a very dynamic sector with new capital-raising initiatives: for example, insurance-linked securities (ILS) or catastrophe bonds (cat bonds). We have seen the appearance of new companies and substantial improvements in pricing and terms in catastrophe premiums for property, marine and energy. The trend shown in Graph 1 demonstrates that natural catastrophes are on the increase in today's world[22]. In addition, reinsurers have developed new protection programs and retrocessional coverage, as well as more prudent underwriting, instead of the chronic underpricing of the 1990s.

Perhaps the most important success of the reinsurance sector has been its "support" of the capital markets, explained by excellent financial security ratings, with 46% of reinsurers in the "A" rating of Standard & Poor's, up to 20% in "AA" rating in 2006, and only 4% below BBB[23]. Another important factor is global reinsurance capital, which hit $575 billion in 2014; this is mainly classified as traditional capital and increasing alternative capital (ILS and cat bonds). This capital has increased in a substantial way: in 2006 it was "only" $385 billion, giving a 66.96% increment between 2006 and 2014[24].

---

21 Cecil Edward Golding (1927), *Sterling Offices Limited: A History of Reinsurance, with Sidelights on Insurance: Offered as a memento of fifty years' service in the reinsurance world*, London, Printed for private circulation by Waterlow & Sons Ltd. Edwin W. Kopf, FCAS (1929), "The Origin and Development of Reinsurance", *Proceedings of the Casualty Actuarial Society*, XVI. Robin Pearson (1995), "The Development of Reinsurance Markets in Europe during the Nineteenth Century", *Journal of European Economic History*, 43:2, pp. 557-72. Harold James, Peter Borscheid, David Gugerli and Tobias Strauman, *The Value of Risk. Swiss Re and the History of Reinsurance*, Oxford, Oxford University Press.

22 In 1988 Hurricane Gilbert ($0.8 billion), in 1989 Hugo ($4.5 billion), in 1992 Andrew ($17 billion), in 2004 Charley ($8.0 billion), also that year Frances ($6.0 billion), Ivan ($12.5 billion) and Jeanne ($5.0 billion) and in 2005, Katrina ($40.0-60.0 billion), Rita ($5.0-10.0 billion) and Wilma ($10.0-15.0 billion). Source: Munich Re.

23 *Global Reinsurance Highlights* (2006), New York, Standard & Poor's Ratings Services, a part of McGraw Hill Financial Inc., p. 11.

24 Global reinsurance capital: the split between traditional and alternative – Source: Aon Benfield.

Graph 1: Great Natural Disasters 1980–2008

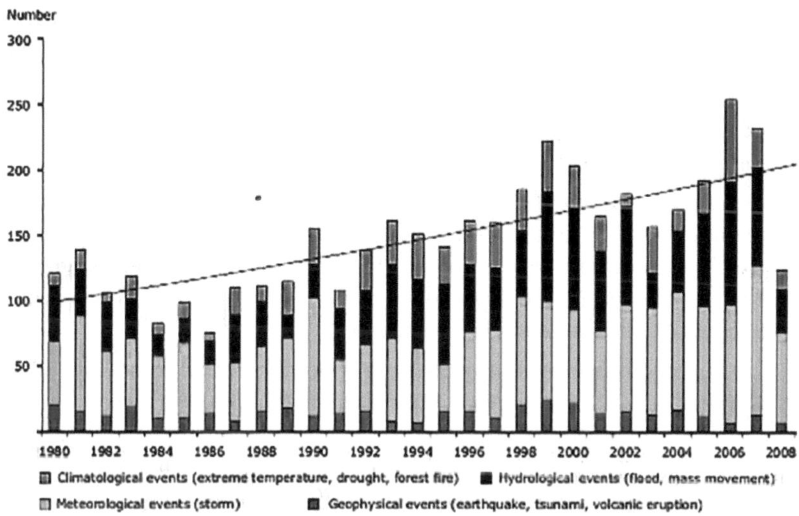

Source: Münchener Rückversicherungs-Gesellschaft, Geo Risks Research, NatCatSERVICE (2010).

The company names that figure in the business of reinsurance over the last decades are mostly the same ones. There have been some important losses in UK, an increase of the relevance of others (e.g., the French company SCOR) and very few new companies in the US[25] (in spite of the fact that it is the most important market in reinsurance). The most dynamic reinsurance locality in the world is the British overseas territory of Bermuda. It was discovered by the Spanish captain Juan de Bermúdez in 1503 and today is one of the richest places in the world, with an average income of $86,000 GDP per capita (2011). Bermuda is an offshore financial center, with little regulation and no direct taxation. This British territory has its own currency, formerly the Bermudian pound, changed in 1970 to Bermudian dollar. The insurance and reinsurance companies have developed offices in Bermuda at several crucial points in time in response to extremes in price performance, following the depletion of worldwide reinsurance capital, with the most extraordinary losses occurring in the property & casualty sectors. The most important developments in the Bermudan reinsurance business occurred after well-known disasters: Hurricane Andrew in August 1992; the terrorist attack of September 11,

[25] The great exception is The Berkshire Hathaway Reinsurance Group.

2001; and the last consecutive hurricanes to hit the US, Katrina, Rita and Wilma (2005).

In 2014 out of the 40 major reinsurance companies in the world, 15 were in Bermuda, totaling $28,434 million net reinsurance premiums written; however, all of these have less than Swiss Reinsurance Company, which in that year netted $31,640 million[26]. The biggest reinsurance company in Bermuda, PartnerRe, is part of a financial group name EXOR S.p.A., controlled by the Agnelli Family. The second largest, Everest Reinsurance Co. Bermuda, is a spin off from Prudential of the US and obviously the greatest part of its business lies in United States. The free movement of capital, and especially lack of taxation, makes this market very attractive for the reinsurance industry[27].

Ultimately, however, the overriding motivator for the location of a reinsurance business is the need to position itself in proximity to the main insurance companies and their clients.

Table 1: Top 10 Companies in 1994 and in 2014. Ranked by Net Reinsurance Premiums Written (Mil, $)

Munich Re	11,979	Swiss Re	31,640.0
Swiss Re	9,297	Munich Re	31,180.9
Cologne Re[28]	3,551	Berkshire Hathaway Re	16,568.0
Employers Re	3,484	Hannover Rueckversicherung AG	15,293.5
Hannover Re	3,228	SCOR SE	12,324.0
General Re	3,001	Lloyd's	10,415.7
Gerling[29]	2,661	Reinsurance Group of America, Inc.	8,669.9
Generali	2,249	China Reinsurance (Group) Corp	7,771.9
Mercantile & General[30]	1,973	PartnerRe Ltd. Bermuda	5,719.9
Frankona Re[31]	1,908	Everest Reinsurance Co. Bermuda	5,256.9

Source: Global Reinsurance Highlights (2015).

26 Global Reinsurance Highlights (2015), p. 58.

27 The annual Everest Re report for 2015 states: "Under Bermuda law, no income, withholding or capital gains taxes are imposed upon Group and its Bermuda subsidiaries. Group and its Bermuda subsidiaries have received an undertaking from the Minister of Finance in Bermuda that, in the event of any taxes being imposed, Group and its Bermuda subsidiaries will be exempt from taxation in Bermuda until March 2035. Non-Bermuda branches of Bermuda subsidiaries are subject to local taxes in the jurisdictions in which they operate."

28 Acquired by General Re in 1995; General Re acquired by Berkshire Hathaway in 1998.

29 Gerling and Generali withdrawn from third-party reinsurance, date not known.

30 Acquired by Swiss Re in 1996.

31 Acquired by Employers Re in 1995.

Among the main strategic moves in the reinsurance market we can mention the acquisition in 1996 by Munich Re of American Re at a cost of $3,300 million and the purchase by Swiss Re of Mercantile & General Reinsurance Co. Ltd, one of the last UK specialist reinsurers.

Less Well-known Markets

The relevance of Europe is indisputable, but other parts of the world have excellent markets of reinsurance. This is the case in Australia and New Zealand. In the overall statistics these two countries are placed with Asia (mainly Japan, Korea, China and India) in the league of reinsurance companies that are major players in the world market. In 2014 seven of the most important reinsurance groups in the world (40) were from these regions[32]. The enormous capability of this part of the world is proved because even when they suffered significant losses (e.g., the Tohoku earthquake, the Japanese tsunamis, and the Christchurch earthquakes in New Zealand), they still maintained strong credit ratings and sought risk in the US or other countries to diversify risk portfolios.

Finally, the market has been growing steadily in the last decade, as is shown in Graph 2 (growth since the beginning of the 21st century). Germany and Switzerland represent 43% of the share of global reinsurance capacity. London is apparently only 8.6%, but is far more important because a great part of the business is developed there through brokers and intermediaries. America is 15.6%, although it should be more as it is the most important insurance market. Bermuda is 11.3% and Asia/the Pacific region practically the same with 11.1%[33].

32 The 11th in the world league is the Korean Reinsurance Co. with 3,582 (Net reinsurance premiums written (Mil. $)); 13th is MS&AD Holdings (Japan) with 3,320; 14th is Sompo Japan Nipponkoa Holdings Inc. with 2,853; 16th is the famous Tokio Marine Group with 2,496. The first Indian company in reinsurance is 18th on the world league, the General Ins. Corp. of India, 2,216; 23rd is Toa Re Co. Ltd. of Japan with 1,746; and the 24th is QBE Insurance Group Ltd. of Australia with 1,571 (Net reinsurance premiums written (Mil. $).

33 *A. M. Best. Global Reinsurance-Segment Review* (September 2014).

Graph 2: Growth since the Beginning of the 21st Century

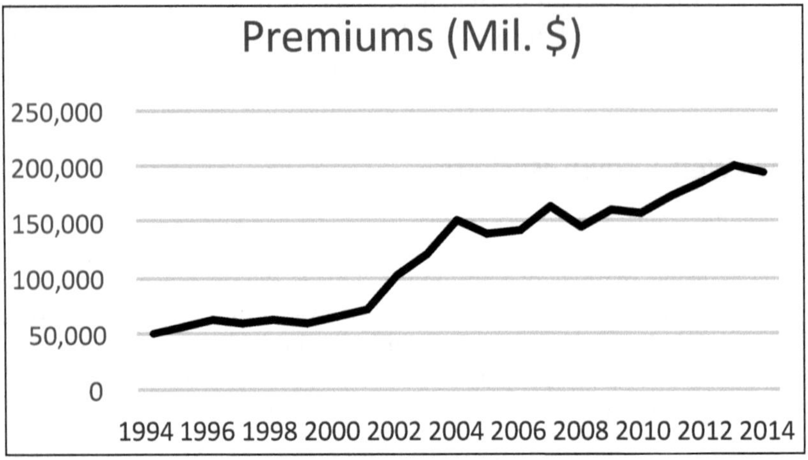

Source: Global Reinsurance Highlights. From 1995 to 2015. Net reinsurance premiums written (NRPW). All, non-life and life reinsurance[34].

34 *This information is about list legal entities, not consolidated groups. In addition, some of the companies that have reinsurance and insurance do not provide complete information about reinsurance.*

Interview with José Manuel Martinez, President of Honor of MAPFRE

Leonardo CARUANA DE LAS CAGIGAS

1. *In your opinion what were the most difficult decisions for MAPFRE in the early years of the birth and development of the business of reinsurance?*

The 1980s was overwhelmed with very difficult decisions. Starting with the creation of MAPFRE Reinsurance in 1981. First based on the firm conviction that for MAPFRE was essential to begin its international expansion. Second, the huge enthusiasm developed by a small team of young managers, who created MAPFRE Services Reinsurance in 1975 (a small department pioneer in this business). What was crucial that we had the illusion that Spain in a short future will have a reasonably important international reinsurer company in the context of the global reinsurance market. However, above all or in addition, we had the vision of making reinsurance differently, it was call reinsurance with soul. We offered not only the necessary risk-taking by the reinsurer, which was the traditional, but also services such as product development, training, strategic experiences, etc. based on the experiences of our own insurance group, which was already an example, although incipient successful in direct insurance.

In reinsurance business we had a very rapid development and in the year 1984, only three years after the creation of MAPFRE RE, we established the first office abroad, in Mexico City. This decision was important for what it meant for a company that until then had only presence and employees in Spain. A year after the opening of this office, did happen a terrible earthquake in Mexico that affected mainly the Federal District and was one of the worst natural disasters in that country. For MAPFRE RE, it had a significant economic impact that was supported by the whole group. At that time we decided something very important for the future of MAPFRE RE, we solve our financial commitments fast and in an exemplary way. I even personally went to the city of Mexico to make it easier for payment to our ceding companies.

That decision had a major impact on the Latin American insurance companies, despite its great youth, MAPFRE RE was an example of rapid and effective action. I will always remember the FIDES meeting of that year (international insurance organization that brings large number of insurers and reinsurers). When I and Lorenzo Garagorri (responsible for this business area) we were at a restaurant, all the people stood up and we receive a long applause. This decision of being fast in payment to the insurance companies, somehow, was a milestone for our future, and thanks to it, our reputation grew and spread fast.

Another important decision that year was the integration of MAPFRE Reinsurance in MAPFRE Corporation, which thus became a reinsurer. MAPFRE Corporation was a subsidiary of MAPFRE Mutualidad and had the property of the entire insurance group. In addition, that was a clear sign of the great support for the reinsurance business. This decision was not without criticism from the market that did not understand why MAPFRE bet so strong, with so much courage and confidence in reinsurance risk, and with operations mainly in Latin America that was not in their best moments. This decision created distrust from investors and other reinsurers, who saw the birth of a competitor. Even in the board of MAPFRE, some executives criticize the international business because things in the local market were developing so well and did not consider necessary to assume risk abroad. Those executives who thought so were wrong. I have always defended and recommended the international expansion, it is desirable to develop when things are going well, because then you can better cope the economic difficulties which usually involves making new operations in other countries. The learning process is always tough, plus is far better to develop international strategy when it is a vocation. From a strategic point of view it must develop because domestic operations do provide excellent results, and not as a way forward when you do not grow in the internal market.

In that same decade, in 1986, we open an office in Manila. This city will be our entrance door in the Far East. In Europe, we open offices in Lisbon and Milan. Finally, with the creation of MAPFRE XL we specialize in operations in the reinsurance segment called not proportional, so important for the development of MAPFRE Reinsurance.

The last important decisions of this decade will be the acquisitions in 1989, 8 years after the creation of MAPFRE RE, of the reinsurer Caja de Chile and CIAR. The first was one of the great companies in Latin American. This company started as a state company, which monopolize reinsurance business and acquired a large size and prestige. I remember in the mid-1980s when we visited the company; it was very difficult that they receive us, even if we had the purpose to participate in its reinsurance contracts (retrocessions). Undoubtedly, we had the feeling that we were visiting an excellent company. Subsequently this company privatized, first, by placing its shares between Chileans insurers and secondly, opened the possibility that the shareholders were from foreign companies. That was a great opportunity for MAPFRE. We took advantage that we were well considered in this market, and we bought all the shares of the reinsurer at a very good price. With this operation, we significantly increased our size and our prestige. It was the first major acquisition of MAPFRE abroad and did indicated the path for the internationalization of MAPFRE.

The other operation was the acquisition of a major stake in CIAR, European reinsurer. It was the culmination of a long and close cooperation exchange. This cooperation was in direct insurance business with European mutuals, which had begun in the 1970s. It was very satisfying to see that this group of mutuals, most of them bigger than MAPFRE when we started those exchanges, granted the leadership to MAPFRE of this project to the point that some of them later took minority stakes in the capital of MAPFRE RE. Moreover, it was our entrance in Europe, an area with great know how, with large companies and experience in insurance and reinsurance.

This period of great activity and permanent decisions culminates with the acquisition in the heart of London City of a magnificent building for the immediate opening of an office in the largest international reinsurance market in the world. I remember it was propose by Andres Jimenez; he was the General Manager of MAPRE RE. Who with great vision and entrepreneurship took the risk of this decision.

2. The easiest decision

In the business world, there is always the risk of being wrong. Decisions are easier depending on the experience of people or in some cases because they obey strategic reasons. In the case of reinsurance, was very clear that international expansion was essential for MAPFRE. We knew we would have to overcome many problems, economical problems as internal and external, but when you have such a clear objective, everything is easier.

3. The least profitable decision

Undoubtedly, we have made wrong decisions that have an economic cost for MAPFRE, but fortunately most had reported a profit. In my opinion, all decisions have long-term profitability even if you are wrong. In some cases, it is important to know that you are doing a mistake and quickly rectify and learn from it. Like that, you do not do the mistake again. What is not profitable in the business world is that you do not take decisions. Which leads you to stagnation and disappears as a company. Although still worse than no decision, is take one with criteria other than professional decisions, as recently happened in some sectors in Spain, where political factors have been decisive in business performance.

4. The greatest achievement

I think the development of reinsurance did fulfil its own operations, but in addition has develop MAPFRE in the foreign markets and widely has contributed to its importance today. As for the reinsurer business, it seems to me almost a miracle MAPFRE RE. I think it is a unique case; it took place in a context and in a business with so many difficulties that led to the disappearance in Spain of some reinsurers who were born at the same time or even before MAPFRE RE. For example CERSA (subsidiary of La Unión y El Fénix Español the Spanish largest insurer at the time). REUNISA (founded by many Spanish insurance companies as a reinsurer). Goya (subsidiary of the company La Estrella), Albatros, etc. Finally, also some of the well know companies with international prestige, which once had been a model for us when we started, as in the case of the Mercantile & General (largest reinsurer in UK), SARF of France, UNIORIAS of Italy or Nationale-Nederlanden from Holland.

It is obvious that in business, miracles do not exist; in our case, have probably been a concatenation of favorable circumstances and wise decisions that have been the reasons for this great business success. However, if I had to highlight some, I would say, on the one hand, membership and the support of all the MAPFRE Group, especially at the beginning, and the success with people. I will not mention names but people who started directly or indirectly reinsurance activity and I am talking about few people have ended up being Chairman or Vice-Chairman of MAPFRE. The great development since the 1980s has a name the President of MAPFRE RE, Andres Jimenez, whose work also continued in an extraordinary way the current Chairman, Pedro de Macedo, and the General Director, Eduardo Perez de Lema.

No one who began MAPFRE Reinsurance thought that only just over 30 years later that MAPFRE RE would be among the 15 largest reinsurers in the world. With a recognized prestige worldwide, with premiums reaching 3,343 million euros, with funding own that reach 1,179 million and a profit of more than 200 million euros.

I would like to emphasize the importance of being a company of the MAPFRE Group. Because the business is based on principles and values, which generates a sense of belonging to all who work in the company, that I think it is the biggest and best motivation for people to develop a job well done and with dedication and enthusiasm, which is the basis of business success.

5. The most serious error

It was before the creation of MAPFRE RE, following what was then the fashion in the market, and due to the lack of experience in the reinsurance business. We arranged permission to underwrite reinsurance business on our behalf to international agencies, which in some cases were fraudulent. This affected us economically because at that time we were small. This pushed us even more to the need of developing reinsurance business. Moreover, this is an example of what I mentioned earlier, we learned of the error and never we fell into one of these and like that, we probably prevented larger problems when MAPFRE RE was a bigger company.

6. *Other considerations regarding decision-making*

In this business, decision-making is daily and you have to constantly assume a risk and by what amount you assume your risk. It is based on criteria of experience, technical and professionals, these are the roots for success in reinsurance business. Finally, the more complicated decisions are those concerning people, but when you're wrong you have to have a strong will to rectify although it is very costly emotionally for the person who makes the decision and to who is affected by it.

The Impact of Reinsurance upon Marine and Fire Insurance Markets in Japan, 1890-1923

How the First Mover Did Build its Organizational Capabilities by Making Use of Reinsurance Network?

Takau YONEYAMA

Introduction and aim of this chapter

In the early stage of marine insurance market in Japan, reinsurance market was important for strengthen its competitiveness of marine insurers. In the 1880s no significant fire insurance companies had been in Japan, partly because of just before the industrialization and partly because of the pre urbanization period. So the presence of marine insurance stood out in insurance market before 1900.

There were three important marine insurers in the 1890s, although some small local companies mainly played in coastal and inland marine insurance business. Actually Tokio Marine was the first modern insurance company in Japan. It established in 1879, and the company had been the only 'national' marine insurance company until the followers were established in 1893. The followers were Nihon Kairiku (Japan Marine and Inland) and Teikoku Marine (Imperial Marine). Especially the capital of Nihon Kairiku was larger than Tokio Marine, and it was strongly supported by the Nippon Life which was one of the largest life insurers in Japan.

By the way, Tokio Marine faced at financial difficulties in the early business. Such difficulties were overcome by the Governmental supports. It was natural for the Government that the only national marine insurance company was an important device for promoting the foreign trade. These difficulties partly caused by its immature insurance skills and a lack of insurance experts. The company employed excellent graduates from Tokyo College of Commerce. By the late 1880s, Tokio Marine tried to expand its business into foreign markets. The results from foreign markets were satisfactory at the beginning. However, beginner's luck does not keep doing. The results gradually became worse in the early 1890s.

It was such a time that new marine insurance companies entered the market. The both followers comparatively had strong financial bases, Nihon Kairiku was supported by Nippon Life, and Teikoku Marine was supported by Yasuda Zaibatsu (family-based enterprise group).

The good results from foreign market seemed to be fascinating for the followers, because of opportunities for new entrants with comparatively strong capital and small connections with marine insurance brokers. Although the directors of Tokio Marine recognized an omen of disaster from the results of foreign business by 1893, the Nihon Kairiku entered the foreign business without proper insurance skills. It was not easy for Nihon Kairiku to get good results in foreign business, and the huge losses from foreign business raised the company insurmountable difficulty by 1900.

Tokio Marine tried to find some way of escaping bankrupt. Teikoku Marine kept a prudent strategy on foreign business, so the foreign results did not cause serious problems. Tokio Marine got lessons by the troubles. After finding a way out of terrible difficult results in foreign business, Tokio Marine was recognized a reliable marine insurer by Lloyd's brokers. It was mainly owed upon a young director who recruited as a manager from the Tokyo College of Commerce. He was an excellent manager, and Tokio Marine would build its organizational capabilities under his directorship. Finally Tokio Marine had built a reputation of an important marine insurer in the world.

Nihon Kairiku finally went bankrupt in 1903. It was unfortunately for the company that the first Insurance Business Act enacted in 1900. The act required insurance company to make stronger reserve than one by previous regulation, but Nihon Kairiku failed to add anything to the reserve fund. Teikoku Marine survived, but it failed to accumulate its experience points from foreign business.

Although a new marine insurance company entered the market in 1898, the Tokio Marine had already built its first mover's advantage in marine insurance business in Japan. There were some factors for building its organizational capability. Out of these factors, reinsurance accessibility was the most important. Tokio Marine seemed to be recognized an important player in international marine insurance market, after solving the troubles of foreign business owing to its excellent young manager.

In the meanwhile, the newly established marine insurers established after 1900. They found their connection to international network in order to catch up with the first mover. Some companies successfully made reinsurance contracts. For example, Kobe Marine contracted with Swiss Re in

1914[1]. It is the first reinsurance contract for Swiss Re with Japanese marine insurers[2]. It was a key factor for competitiveness in marine insurance market that they could reinsure their business by international market.

By the way, competition in fire business became stronger than one before 1900, partly because of the rapid growth of the number of fire insurance companies. Fire insurers sometimes tried to make collusion. But the early trials almost failed. On the contrary, marine insurance business suddenly enjoyed a brisk market by shipping boom of the First World War. Although marine premiums went up rapidly together with substantial rise of the price of a ship, the claims were not so large amount which they had expected. In pursuit of profits, some marine insurance companies established and many fire insurers expanded its business into marine, but Tokio Marine only realized extraordinary returns, and the others got a gain as a side effect. Tokio Marine expanded its business into fire insurance business in 1914 for the first time. Consequently strong leadership of Mr. Kenkichi Kagami, a director of Tokio Marine, enables to establish tariff organization in 1917. As a result, marine and fire markets in Japan became stable.

The stability suddenly was destroyed by the Great Earthquake in 1923. At that time, the reinsurance did not work because of insurance wordings, but reinsurance contracts became to be more important than the period before the Great earthquake, because almost all non-life insurance company fallen to financial weakness by the payment of enforced 10% of insurance money as a gift to earthquake suffered. As Tokio Marine only had a strong connection to foreign market, the company strengthened its position in marine and fire insurance market in Japan.

We focused on the period between 1890 and 1923 in this chapter. The history of Japanese insurance shows what the most important factors for creating organizational capability in the early non-life insurance business were. In short, marine was a key business in insurance, and building of insurance network with foreign market was the most important factor for creating organizational capability for non-life insurance company.

Researches and Sources

In Japan, we have lots of company histories edited by the companies themselves in each industry. It is not exceptional in insurance industry. Almost all insurance companies have published their company history, and some ones are very bulky. Each history refers to the reinsurance business, but we cannot

---

1 Dowa Fire and Marine Insurance Company, Ltd. (1995), *The 50 Years History of Dowa Fire, a Complete History*, Dowa Fire and Marine Insurance Company, p. 65.

2 Swiss Re (2013), *A History of Insurance in Japan*, Zurich, Swiss Re, p. 26-27.

help saying that these references did not make clear of how the reinsurance business created their competitiveness or not. Every company history usually recognized the reinsurance business was a means of transfer uninsurable risks. However, reinsurance was not only risk transfer device but also strategic one.

In fact, international experience by means of reinsurance contracts built the organizational capability in insurance business. Although each company history did not clearly refer to the fact, the structure of marine and fire insurance business drastically changed between 1890 and 1923 having been influenced with global insurance business connection including reinsurance. From the point of views, company histories of Tokio Marine, Yasuda Fire, Taisho Marine and Sumitomo Marine, were informative[3].

Kamiya examined the market structure of marine business and clarified the change of the structure before the Second World War[4]. The chapter makes contribution to clarify the structural change in the fire and marine insurance market in Japan, but it does not make a total sketch of the structural changes especially including fire business. Yoneyama have showed the structural changes in both fire and marine markets after the Great Kanto Earthquake, but it does not make a detail examination on the changes before

---

[3] Official company histories were written by Japanese. Tokio Marine has already published 4 official company histories. Tokio Marine and Fire Insurance Company, Ltd., *The 60 Years History* (1940), Tokio, Tokio Marine and Fire Insurance Company, Ltd. *The 80 Years History of Tokio Marine* (1964), Tokio, Japan Business History Institute (ed.). *The Centenary History of Tokio Marine and Fire Insurance, Ltd.*, (1979), Tokio, Japan Business History Institute, (ed.) 1 and 2, (1982), and *The 125 Years History of Tokio Marine,* (2005). Yasuda Fire is a core company of the Sompo Japan Nipponkoa Insurance Inc. The following two official company histories are important. *Yasuda Fire and Marine Insurance Company, Ltd., The 80 Years History,* (1968), Tokio: Yasuda Fire and Marine Insurance Company, Ltd., *The Centenary History of Yasuda Fire,* (1990). Taisho Marine changed its name into Mitsui Marine in 1991. After amalgamation with Sumitomo Marine in 2001, it is a major member of MS & AD Holdings. As for Taisho Marine, Taisho Marine and Fire Insurance Company, Ltd., *The 40 Years History* (1961), Tokio, Japan Business History Institute, (ed.), *The 75 Years History of Mitsui Marine and Fire Insurance* (1996), Tokio: Mitsui Marine and Fire Insurance. The Sumitomo Marine published an official company history (1995), Tokio, Japan Business History Institute (ed.), *The Centenary History of Sumitomo Marine and Fire Insurance* (1995). In addition, they published a brief company history respectively in English. These are as follows; Tokio Marine and Fire Insurance Company, Ltd. (1980), *The Tokio Marine & Fire Insurance, 1879-1979, The First Century.* Yasuda Fire and Marine Insurance Company Ltd. (1980), *The Yasuda Fire and Marine Insurance, 1888-1988, A Century of Achievement* (1988), Mitsui Marine & Fire Insurance Co. Ltd., *Building Protection, The Story of Mitsui Marine & Fire Insurance 1918-1993,* 1994, Sumitomo Marine & Fire Insurance Co. Ltd., *Sumitomo Marine & Fire Insurance, The First Century, 1893-1993,* 1993.

[4] Hisaaki Kamiya (2010), "The emergence of competition in the Japanese marine insurance business and the premium cartel", *Keiei Shigaku (Japanese Business History Review),* 44/4 and "The background on the formation of the Union for Hull Insurers, Japanese marine insurance business in the 1920s" (2012), *Songai-hoken Kenkyu (Review of General Insurance),* 74/3.

the big hit of the Earthquake[5]. Yoneyama gave an outline of particulars of foreign connection with Japanese insurance businesses[6]. The collections of insurance documents before the 1920s were very helpful for insurance historians[7]. A few insurance news and journals began to publish in 1900s[8].

Overseas expansion and its results; different strategies among the three Marine

From 1879 to 1893, Tokio Marine had been the only marine insurance company for oceangoing vessels in Japan, though some small local enterprises insured coastal and inland marine insurance in a tradition way. The followers appeared in 1893. These are Nihon Kairiku (Japan Marine and Inland) and Teikoku Marine (Inperial Marine). Nihon Marine started in 1896 as the fourth marine insurers in Japan[9].

Tokio Marine had already started its foreign business and reinsurance contract some years before the followers had established. Nihon Kairiku immediately followed foreign strategy of Tokio Marine, but the Teikoku Marine did not so. The foreign business and reinsurance network were fascinating to newly established company with large capital. Actually, Nihon Kairiku had twice as large capital as Tokio Marine. Teikoku Marine was not aggressive on the foreign business, because of not only capital structure but also strategy of the top management. Such a strategy was explained by insurance skills and knowledge. The Teikoku Marine recruited Mr. Haruo Mourase as a director. He studied marine insurance at Belgium commercial school, after graduated from the Tokyo College of Commerce[10].

By the way, Tokio Marine became aware of abnormality in foreign business soon. They recognized hull insurance underwritten by London agency suffered a huge loss. As the hull insurance was 50% of total premium

---

5 Takau Yoneyama (2009), "The Great Kanto Earthquake and the Response of Insurance Companies: A Historical Lesson on the Impact of a Major Disaster", *Hitotsubashi Journal of Commerce and Management*, 43/1.

6 Takau Yoneyama (2012), "Japan: The Role of Insurance in the Rapid Modernization of Japan", in Borscheid and Haueter (eds.), *World Insurance: The Evolution of a Global Risk Network*, Oxford, Oxford University Press.

7 The Association of Life Insurance Companies in Japan, *The Meiji Taisho Hoken Shiryo (Insurance Documents in the period of Meiji and Taisho)*, 4/9, 1934-1943.

8 Hoken-Ginko Jiho (*Post Magazine of Insurance and Banking*) is a useful periodical on insurance business, it published from 1904.

9 Yoneyama (2012), p. 499.

10 Yasuda Fire and Marine Insurance Company (ed.) (1988), *The 80 Years History Yasuda Fire and Marine Insurance Company*, Tokyo, Yasuda Fire and Marine Insurance Company, p. 125-126.

income, it was serious problem for Tokio Marine. Tokio Marine finally decided to send a young manager, Mr. Kenkichi Kagami, to London for investing the cause of huge loss and making a settlement of these losses in 1894[11]. He graduated a head of Tokyo College of Commerce[12], and employed Tokio Marine in 1891 by the principal's recommendation. Since he had an excellent talent for insurance management, the company should fill up his vacancy when he visited in London. The company successfully recruited another young man who was graduated from the Tokyo College of Commerce as well[13]. He, Mr. Hachisaburo Hirao, became a marine insurance expert soon, and filled his role at Mr. Kagami's absence in home business. Owing to his recruitment, Mr. Kagami could concentrate into making a research on causes of losses in London free from anxiety on home business.

When we examine the distribution of net profit in the early stage, we cannot help saying that top management of Tokio Marine did not understand insurance business. It was critical for its management that they did not understand the distinguishing feature of insurance debt. Clearly contrasting, young managers studied the modern way of management and its accounting system, and understood the special feature of insurance business soon[14].

Owing to excellent jobs of young managers, Tokio Marine strengthened its competitiveness in marine insurance business. After the settlement of losses, Tokio Marine became to build good connection with Wills Feber, the first-ranked London broker, Mr. Kagami had successfully gotten 'Cargo Cover' in London market, which had been a treaty reinsurance arrangement between Tokio Marine and London underwriters. The Cover was essential for strengthen the competitiveness in marine market in Japan[15].

---

11 Yoneyama (2012), p. 499.

12 The college developed to Tokyo University of Commerce in 1920. The University is the forerunner of Hitotsubashi University. See Makoto Ikema, Yoshio Inoue, Tamotsu Nishizawa and Susumu Yamauchi (eds.), (2000), *Hitotsubashi University 1875-2000, A Hundred and Twenty-Five Years of Higher Education in Japan*, London, MacMillan.

13 Nihon Kairiku would like to employ Mr. Hirao as well. Mr. Hirao wrote in his autobiography. Mr. Kataoka invited him to a spree at a restaurant in the gay quarters, and asked him to join the company. On the contrary, Mr. Kagami zealously asked to join his company in his boarding room with talking each other overnight. Mr. Hirao did not select a kind of traditional way, but he accepted a substantial proposal with pleasure. Hirao, Hachisaburo (Anzai, T. revised), (1996), *Hirao Hachisaburo Jiden (The Autobiography of Hirao Hachisaburo)*, Nagoya, Japaness edition, p. 155-160.

14 Hachisaburo Hirao strongly recruited by a chairman of Nihon Kairiko, when he was a lecturer at Kobe Commercial School. Almost the same time, Jiro Yano, a principle of Tokyo Commercial College, recommended being a manager of Tokio Marine. Hirao was graduated from Tokyo Commercial College (the forerunner of Hitotsubashi University). According to his diary, the chairman of Nihon Kairiku invited him to a traditional restaurant with geisha girl, but Tokio Marine made a meeting where they explained why they needed him. He decided to select Tokio Marine. It is impressive that he disliked conventional business and select modern style business.

15 Yoneyama (2012), p. 500.

Nihon Kairiku had almost as double capital as Tokio Marine, and the company was in a great hurry for catching up with Tokio Marine. Nihon Kairiku fallen into a deep spot in foreign business, partly because of luck of managerial capability. The company recruited no young managers, and in fact, the managers they were sent to London for making rearrangement of huge losses. However, it was too late to revive their business. Moreover, the director was despotic, and the young managers did not have delegated power to cope with trouble in foreign business.

In the meantime, the authority forced Nihon Kairiku to disclose the exact amount of losses under the first Insurance Business Act. The Insurance Business Act and its related laws enforced to make insurance reserve strong against every insurance company. Before Insurance Business Act, the director hoped to manage to solve financial trouble with capital. However, as the stipulations on insurance reserve were much stricter than he had expected, the company recognized they did not have the huge capital. Finally, the company went into liquidation in 1903[16].

By contrast with Nihon Kairiku, Teikoku Marine had not serious losses from foreign business. We have already said as well; the director was fond of prudent strategy. The company paradoxically failed to build organizational capability from experience of trouble of foreign business. The director had a background in European insurance education, actually graduated from Belgium commercial college. He was cautious for expanding foreign business at that time. His aim was that his company will be an excellent and stable marine insurer in Japan with the support of Yasuda Zaibatsu[17].

In summing up the story of the big three in marine insurance business, Nihon Kairiku did not have managerial capability but capital. On the contrary, Tokio Marine did not have enough capital but its managerial capability. Teikoku Marine had both managerial capability and capital, but the company did not decide to select a strategy for expanding its business abroad. Tokio Marine could only build connection with an influential London broker, and the company made a treaty, reinsurance arrangement with London underwriters. The Cover was essential for the competitiveness in marine market in Japan.

16 The details of liquidation of Nihon Kairiku are simply explained in *The 60 Years History of Tokio Marine*, (1940), p. 326-327.

17 Haruo Mourase was a director of Teikoku Marine. He graduated from Tokyo Commercial College as well. He gave lectures on marine insurance at his alma mater. Because he knew well theory and practice in insurance business, he may take a prudent strategy. It was sure that Teikoku Marine expanded its business into foreign insurance. But the company did not make a deep commitment into foreign business. So it is too exaggerated to say 'no strategy'.

The marine insurance market in the 1910s

After 1900, Tokio Marine dominated marine insurance market in Japan thanks to its strong reinsurance cover[18]. The followers as the Teikoku Marine and the Nippon Marine[19] did not have established reinsurance cover from foreign reinsurers.

Actually, reinsurance cover with overseas network was an important condition for entry to marine market in Japan. The followers and new entrants tried to make reinsurance contracts with foreign market. As we have already said, Kobe Marine, newly established company, made a reinsurance contract with Swiss Re in 1914. Although many non-life insurance companies tried to build good connection with foreign reinsurance market, Tokio Marine enjoyed first mover's advantage in reinsurance network.

The break of the First World War changed the marine and fire markets. At first, a great change occurred in Marine business. The price of vessels rapidly was going up, because of shortage of ships for expected war demands. Shipping boom was followed marine insurance prosperity soon. Graph 1 clearly shows the rapid growth of marine insurance premiums in the war time.

Graph 1: Marine and Fire Insurance Premiums of all Companies, 1908-1940

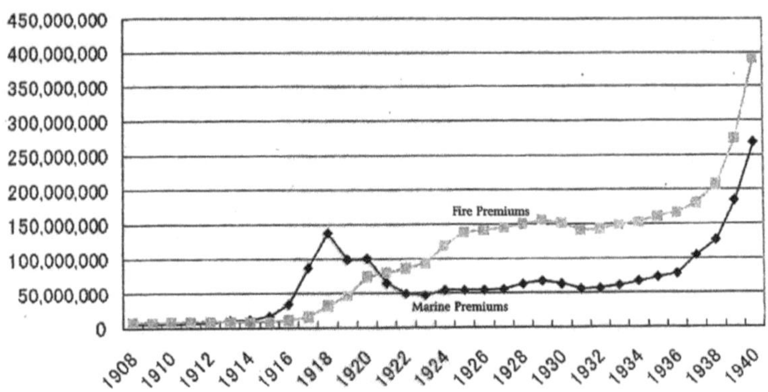

Sources: Yoneyama (2009), p. 22.

Original Sources: The Ministry of Commerce (Previously The Ministry of Agriculture and Commerce) *Hoken Nenkton* (*Insurance Almanack*), each year.

---

18 They called it 'London Cover'. As for the cover, see *The 60 Years History of Tokio Marine* (1940), p. 301-304.

19 Nippon Marine was established in 1896. The founders were mainly ship owners. At first, established three marine excluded Nippon Marine, but gradually it was growing its business. Yoneyama (2012), p. 500.

By the way, marine insurance companies worried about war risks in the First World War. In order to promoting marine insurance contracts in war period, the Government made special legal measures for protecting marine insurance companies against war risks. As a consequence, the damage of war risk was far from being disastrous for marine insurance companies.

Both the result of war risks and the marine insurance boom in the First World War contributed Tokio Marine making the first and probably the last high profit. The followers and new entrants like Kobe Marine did not enjoy enough profits from the marine boom, because their shares were much smaller than Tokio Marine which had strong reinsurance connection with foreign network. Graph 2 shows the marine premium of Tokyo was half of all premium even at the peak of boom in 1918. It is clear that Tokio Marine enjoyed huge profit from marine business.

Graph 2: Marine and Fire Insurance Premiums of Tokio Marine Insurance Company, 1908-1940

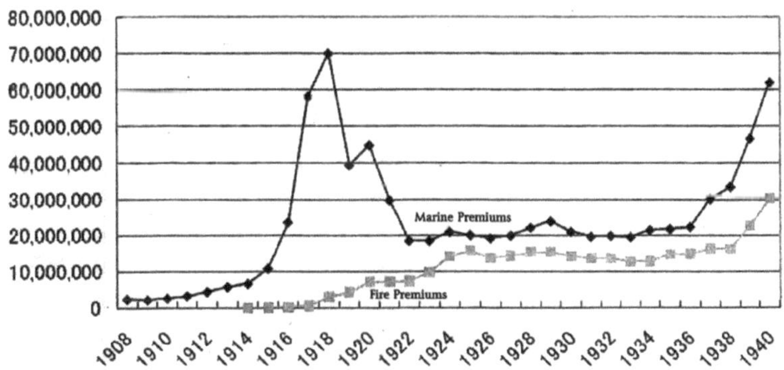

Sources: Yoneyama (2009), p. 22.

Original Sources: The Ministry of Commerce (Previously The Ministry of Agriculture and Commerce) *Hoken Nenkton* (*Insurance Almanack*), each year.

While Tokio Marine got the lion's share of the profits, many marine insurance companies established their financial footings by rest of the share. So the market structure of marine insurance transferred monopoly into oligopoly. Owing to the boom, the premium incomes from marine insurance were surpassed the fire premium incomes. Moreover most of all fire insurance companies expanded its business into marine insurance in this period. The so-called 'composite' insurance companies increased rapidly.

Regarding 'composite', Tokio Marine was not an exception. The company extended its business into fire business in 1914[20]. The decision was explained by redundant fund accumulated by huge profits in a boom. In addition, top manager might think that fire insurance market could make profits if the market could be organized. Although a Japanese representative made an effort to build tariff rates among all insurance companies, the effort was about to be ineffective in 1913. The necessary condition for building tariff rates were that a core company had not only strong leadership but also global reinsurance business network. No man without Mr. Kagami of Tokio Marine would create tariff association for fire insurance. We will examine the process of creating tariff association in the next section.

Tariff organization and a stable market

Mr. Kingo Hara, a director of Meiji Fire, was a plenipotentiary for building a tariff agreement. When Tokio Marine entered fire business, Mr. Kagami was given full powers on tariff agreement pushing away his predecessor. Mr. Hare resigned the Meiji Fire and moved to another fire insurance company.

Tokio Marine was the strongest non-insurance company in Japanese insurance business. Moreover Mr. Kagami had established good reputation as insurance men even in foreign insurers. Owing to these reasons, Mr. Kagami achieved brilliant success for building a tariff organization. Dai-Nippon Rengo Kasai Hoken Kyokai (Japan Fire Coalition Insurance Association, JFCIA) established in 1917[21]. The foreign counterpart followed it soon. And it worked with the JFCIA for making domestic fire insurance market stable. All fire insurance companies without Nihon Kyoritsu Fire joined the JFCIA. At first non-tariff company was only one, and the company was managed by Mr. Hara who moved from the Meiji Fire after dismissing a plenipotentiary for building fire cartel organization[22].

---

20 Tokio Marine was renamed to 'Tokio Marine and Fire' in 1914. But we will write 'Tokio Marine' in this text from first and last.

21 As for the process of forming the organization, there is voluminous book. G. Kon, and Y. Kitazawa (eds.), (1944), *Nihon ni okeru Kasai-hoken Ryoritsu Kyotei Enkakushi* (The History of Tariff Agreement for Fire Insurance in Japan), 1 & 2 (Japanese).

22 Mr. Hara graduated from Tokyo College of Commerce as well. He was older than Mr. Kagami. He openly revealed feelings of antagonism towards Mr. Kagami and Tokio Marine. He worked energetically as a director of a non-tariff company. Kon, G. and Kitazawa, Y. (eds.), (1944), p. 576-577.

Aside the Nihon Kyoritsu Fire as an ordinary fire insurance company, some fire insurance exclusively for movable properties did not join the tariff. Since the amount of insurance of these companies was limited by the regulation, they used to be out of ordinary fire insurance market even before 1916. Although there were some preceding companies in this special small amount fire insurance for the common people, these are very small and abortive ones before 1900. The field did not recognize them as a reliable business until the following three insurance companies for movable properties gained in reputation in the 1920s. Nihon Dosan Fire (Japan Movable Estates Fire) started its business again in 1914[23]. Nihon Kan'i Fire (Japan Small Amount Fire)[24] and Tokyo Dosan Fire were established in 1918[25]. They did not join the JFCIA because they did provide different products for different customers. Consequently non-tariff companies consisted of two ordinary fire insurance companies and three movable estates fire insurance companies in the late 1920[26].

Since fire insurers suffered from excessive price competition in unstable market, the tariff rate association was their heart's desire. Long-cherished desire had been fulfilled, when the JFCIA built in 1916.

While the fire insurance market became stable, fire insurance needs were growing in the 1910s and 1920s. Insurance objects in commercial line increased together with the development of heavy industrialization, Insurable personal houses were also growing along with urbanization.

---

23 The forerunner of the company was a small quasi insurance company established in 1892. As a great fire hit the company, the authority ordered it to stop its business for clearing the debt. The company stopped selling insurance almost 10 years. When the demand for movable fire insurance was raised, the company tried to restart its business after changing the name of the company in 1914. The head office was located on Osaka. *The 40 Years History of Nichido Fire and Marine Insurance Company* (1954) p. 5-51. The company is a forerunner of Tokio Marine & Nichido Fire Insurance Company, Ltd.

24 The company established in Osaka as well. As for the particulars of establishment and its early business, see *Fuji Fire: 70 Years History*, (1989), p. 5-16. This company is a member of AIG Japan Holdings.

25 Contrary to the above two companies, this company established on Tokyo. As to the details of the establishment, see *The 50 Years History: Dai Tokyo Fire and Marine Insurance Company*, 1971. As for the early business of the company, see *The History of Dai Tokyo Fire and Marine Insurance Company* (2004), p. 22-36. This company is a forerunner of Aioi Nissay Dowa Insurance Company Ltd.

26 Another ordinary fire insurance company started its business in Japan Spring 1923. Although Taisei Fire was founded in 1919 under Governor-General of Formosa, the authority delayed the approval of selling fire insurance in homeland. The company managed by Japanese, but most shareholders are Taiwanese. The details of early business were described by the following company histories. *A Brief History of Taisei Fire* (1970), 3-13, and *The 40 Years History of Taisei Fire and Marine Insurance Company* (1991), p. 2-43.

Consequently fire premiums grew as large as marine by 1920, which is shown in the graph I.

Concluding: Creating of Organizational Capability and reinsurance network

In the early non-life insurance market in Japan, Tokio Marine had been a strong leader in the business. Before building its advantage, excellent managers put a troubled Tokio Marine back on its feet, and kept strong connection with foreign brokers and agents. It was very important for Tokio Marine that the company controlled domestic market, where most insurers had not enough connection with world-wide reinsurance contracts. At the same time, Tokio Marine strengthened its managerial capability. Young managers improved its operation into western style, and rationalized the business. They were quick to learn the nature of insurance, and improved its accounts for coordinating insurance business. Moreover, foreign network, especially reinsurance business, was crucial for building advantage in non-life insurance market in this period. Since Tokio Marine built up global network for reinsurance swiftly, this company had created an organizational capability. The capability was explained by its coping with changeable international market and controlling the domestic market under strong advantages both in finance and management.

If we focused on why its organizational capability created, we could find some reasons about Tokio Marine. First, while Tokio Marine got a strong connection with London brokers just after making a settlement of its loss in foreign business, no Japanese companies have a lesson from such an experience in foreign business. Although the followers and new entrants were getting reinsurance connection with foreign market in the 1910s, the first mover's advantage in business connections including reinsurance had been continued until the 1920s.

Second, Tokio Marine fortunately succeeded a huge profit in the boom of shipping market in the First World War. In the beginning of the boom, its share of business among domestic marine insurers was overwhelming majority (See the graph II). Especially for ocean marine, the shares of both Teikoku Marine and Nihon Marine were very small. For the purpose of getting profits from the boom, lots of fire insurers expanded its business into marine insurance and new companies established in the middle of the 1910s. However, the lion's share was obtained by Tokio Marine, and the rests were distributed to the others. Tokio Marine could accumulate a reserve for liability several times as large as legal reserve, but the other fire and marine insurers did not so.

Third, Tokio Marine decided to expand its business into fire insurance in 1914. As the company had the strongest insurance company among non-life insurance business in both finance and underwriting skills, it is natural it would sell fire insurance especially in commercial line. The managers might forecast the following two factors.

Last but not less important, they expected that fire insurance market had been unstable and unprofitable, but it would surely make a profit if the market would be organized well. After entering fire market, Tokio Marine took the initiative in building a cartel organization both in domestic fire insurers and in foreign fire insurance companies. As for the second factor, the managers expected the fire business would be more important than marine after the boom. We can recognize that their expectation came true in the graph I. Fire business of Tokio Marine became important in the business soon, fire business had been occupied about 10% of total fire insurance premium of all fire insurers (See the graph III).

Graph 3: Market Share of Tokio Marine Inscurance Company, 1908-1940

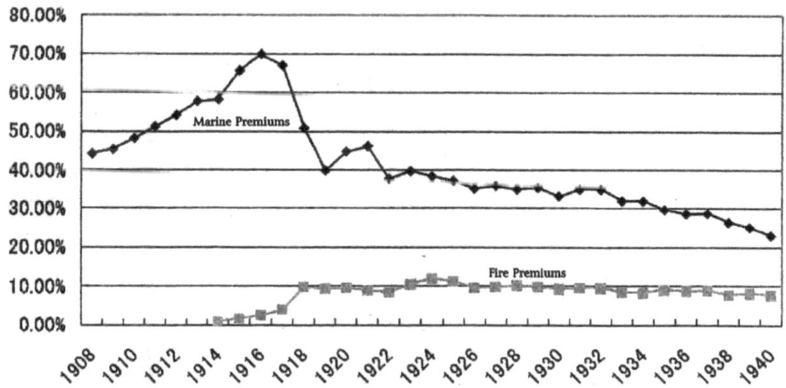

Sources: Yoneyama (2009), p. 23.

Original Sources: The Ministry of Commerce (Previously The Ministry of Agriculture and Commerce) *Hoken Nenkton* (*Insurance Almanack*), each year.

In fact, the fire insurers were damaged by the Great Kanto Earthquake on September 1923. Legally speaking, they had no responsibility to the payment for damage by earthquake, but the payment became to be a political problem. After the prolonged negotiations, it was concluded that the ordinary fire company should make a payment of 10% of insurance money[27]. The foreign fire insurance companies did make repayment of fire premiums. Nearly all fire insurance companies did not pay the 10% payment without the governmental loan. Tokio Marine and the new entrant did make pay the 10% payment without governmental loan. The impact on industrial organization of marine and fire insurance were significant. The result was that the presence of Tokio Marine in the market of marine and fire became much more important. But this did not end in a monopoly of Tokio Marine. On the contrary, the company organized both market well, and the shares did not always increase. The story has already written in my previous article[28].

Japan is an island country of which oceans are surrounded on all sides. It is natural that marine insurance business was more important than the other insurance. At the same time the new Government was eager to promote foreign trade in the opening of the country after the long-continued period of national isolation in Japan. The government supported the first established Japanese insurance company in the early business.

As for the other kind of insurance, life assurance companies were growing for themselves without any governmental supports. Fire insurance companies also developed for themselves. The first fire insurance company, the business of Tokyo Fire was in personal lines, and the second fire insurance company, Meiji Fire was concentrated in factories and warehouses. In their early business, they did not directly have reinsurance cover from foreign market. On the contrary to life and fire, reinsurance was indispensable to marine business, because of its nature. The first mover in insurance business created its organizational capability through foreign business including reinsurance contracts in taking a tortuous course. As for life assurance business, we have totally another story partly because the reinsurance contracts were not always necessary for life assurance business.

We can conclude by saying that the most important factor in Japanese non-life insurance business was global insurance network before the Second World War.

---

27 The 'ordinary' means all fire insurers except for the small amount fire insurers.

28 Yoneyama (2009), p. 11-26.

Global Insurance Market and Sergey Yu. Witte's Economic Policy

Yury Petrov

In November 1894, Russia's Minister of Finance Sergey Yu. Witte addressed to the Minister of Interior Pyotr N. Durnovo asking him to uphold the idea of founding a special company involved in the mutual reinsurance business with a view to reducing dependence of the Russian insurance industry on the global market. "It has been a long time", the letter stated, "since national insurance companies began reinsuring most of their business with other companies of the same kind, but in so doing they have regretfully made their choice almost exclusively in favor of foreign companies. In the meantime, being detrimental to the insurance business as a whole, such an abnormal state of things has a negative impact on the country's general economic interests". "Striving to establish the national insurance industry", Witte reported to have held a meeting with the representatives of thirteen leading Russian fire insurance companies who had accepted his idea. The Minister of Finance suggested to "introduce the issue for consideration by the Committee of Ministers in the nearest future"[1].

Witte's letter laid the foundation of an interesting project enabling us to outline more accurately general framework of Russia's economic policy in the late 19th century. In the course of debates over the Minister of Finance's initiative, a number of materials were prepared containing the data missing in other sources which can substantially complement our entrenched attitudes towards interrelation between the Russian and the global international insurance markets at the turn of the 20th century[2]. Those documents have been found in the Russian State Historical Archive (RGIA) in Saint Petersburg. I express my sincere gratitude to the archive employees Sergey Chernyavsky and Natalia Kolosenkova for their kind assistance.

---

1 S.Yu. Witte – ministru vnutrennikh del I.N. Durnovo, 12 Noyabrya 1894 g. Rossiyskiy Gosudarstvenny Istoricheskiy Arkiv (RGIA). F. 23. Op. 24. D. 234. L. 1-3.

2 Yuri Petrov (2012), "Russia: Early expansion, state involvement, and re-emergence of the insurance industry", in Borscheid and Haueter (eds.), *World Insurance. The Evolution of a Global Risk Network*, Oxford, Oxford University Press, p. 213-238.

Why did Sergey Witte, Russia's Minister of Finance since 1892, care so much for the insurance issue? To begin with, the general direction of his economic policy shall be taken into consideration. As a strong advocate of accelerated industrial growth of his country under the state control and with an active involvement of the foreign capital, Witte undertook a series of essential reforms fostering Russia's rapid industrialization.

The core idea of his economic views and practical activity in the post of Minister of Finance was the creation of the national industry protected from foreign competition by customs barriers. To accomplish this, as the Minister of Finance was convinced, the country needed "capital, know-how and entrepreneurial spirit", wherein the most essential element was capital – both Russian and especially foreign. The procurement of loan and investment capital in the first place was considered by Witte as the backbone of his financial system. "Under the Minister of Finance's profound conviction", he reported to the emperor Nicolas II in 1899, "the inflow of foreign capital is the only way to allow our industry achieve the point where it will manage to supply our country with abundant and cheap goods"[3].

The Witte's system implied the speeding up of the national industry's growth not only by attracting foreign investments, but also by mobilizing domestic resources, raising indirect taxes, establishing a state monopoly on alcohol, augmenting trade and industrial tax burdens. The protectionist customs law of 1891 was supposed to protect the national industry against foreign business rivals. The government was ready to take measures in order to foster the exports of Russian goods[4].

The idea of practically unlimited state participation in the country's economic life laid out the basic foundation for Witte's economic program. He was convinced that under the autocratic rule the accelerated national industrial growth was possible only through an intense exploitation of public sector of the economy and state interference with the economy. "The living conditions in Russia", Witte wrote to Nicolas II in 1895, "have required state interference with widely differing areas of civil life what makes it fundamentally distinct from England, for instance, where

3 Vsepoddanneyshiy doklad ministra finanso S.Yu. Witte o neobkhodimosti ustanovit' i zatem neprelozhno priderzhivat'sya opredelennoy programmy torgovo-promyshlennoy politiki imperii. 1899 g. Materialy po istorii SSSR. T. VI. M., 1959. S. 173-174, 177-178 and 184.

4 For more details on Witte's economic doctrine please refer to: Boris V. Annan'ich, Rafail Sh. Ganelin (1999), *SY Witte and his time*. St Petersburg, Dmitrii Bulanin; Avenir P. Korelin, Stepanov, S. (1998), S.Yu. Witte – finisist, politik, diplomat. Moscow, Terra; Yury A. Petrov (2002), 'Ekonomicheskoe polozhenie imperii v nachale XX', in Yakovleva *v. Rossiya v nachale XX veka.* (The economic situation of the empire at the start of the 20th centuary), Moscow, Noviy khronograf.

everything is moved by private initiative and where the state only regulates private activity"[5]. The State Bank appeared to be an important conductor of the statist policy. In 1894 its new charter was adopted. The Bank reported directly to the Minister of Finance who in fact directed its activity as the main national credit institution[6].

For Witte Russia's economic development was tied together with an active struggle for the markets of Russia's eastern neighboring states. He was hoping that within several years the Russian industry would achieve relatively high level and the Russian manufactured goods would withstand competition in the Middle and Far East markets enabling Russia to repay its western loans using the income from the exports of the Russian manufactured goods to the eastern markets.

Following the doctrine of so-called "peaceful" penetration to the Middle and Far East markets announced by Witte, several banks were founded to become conductors of that policy. In spite of a constant lack of spare capital in the country, Russia began to credit certain countries in the East and in the Balkan Peninsula. The capital export was carried out either directly by the State Bank or with its assistance by commercial banks controlled by the Finance Ministry. The Russo-Chinese Bank and the Discount and Loan Bank of Persia played a special role in pursuing that policy. The former was founded in 1895 and its capital was formed by the Russian government and to a great extent by the French bankers, while the latter was fully owned by the Russian government[7].

For the Minister of Finance the economic growth meant first and foremost maintenance of Russia's great power status and extension of the imperial sphere of influence. "The international competition", he warned Nicolas II in 1900, "is not awaiting. If we do not take energetic and decisive measures immediately so that in the course of the next decades our industry will be able to satisfy the needs of Russia and of the Asiatic countries which are – or should be – under our influence, then the rapidly growing foreign industries will manage to break through our tariff barriers <…> and after driving their roots into the depths of our economy they will be able to gradually clear the way for the more alarming foreign political effects"[8]. However, as the Russo-Japanese War of 1904-1905 later showed, in the immediate future Russia was not destined to gain a foothold in the Far East markets.

---

5 Boris V Annanich (1996), *Vlastì reform at samoderzhavnoi k sovetskoi Rossii* (Authority and reforms. Form autocratic to Soviet Russia), St. Petersburg, p. 416.

6 Yury A. Petrov, S.V. Tatarinov (2010), *Istoriya Banka Rossii. 1860-2010*: v 2, Moscow.

7 Boris V. Annanich (1970), *Rossiia i mezhdunarodnyi Kapital, 1897-1914* (Russia and International capital), Leningrad.

8 Avenir P. Korelin, S. A. Stepanov, S. *Yu. Witte – finisist, politik, diplomat*, p. 66.

Among the key directions of Witte's policy was the movement towards the monometallic monetary system. The system based on silver introduced in Russia in the late 1830s and early 1840s was abolished owing to enormous expenditures for the Crimean War of 1853-1856. During the following forty years Russia used the inflationary paper standard with a highly variable floating exchange rate. It was followed by the gold standard system established by Witte in the course of the currency reform of 1895-1897[9].

In the first place Witte kept in mind external economic aspect, the prospect to attract investments from the economically developed countries to which end stable national currency was needed. "The paramount importance of the gold currency", the Minister of Finance stated his position to the emperor Nicolas II, "lies particularly in the fact that it is like a golden bridge leading from the rich to the poor countries; such a system shortens the road away from poverty whereas the paper currency lengthens it". The reform was designed to set the conditions for intensifying the Russian exports and hindering the imports of manufactured goods to the country and in so doing to activate Russia's international account balance.

With a view to accumulating the gold reserve serving as a basis for the monometallic monetary system, there existed two internal sources – gold extraction and imports intensification. In the late 19th century the volume of gold extraction in Russia remained roughly constant, with the annual income ranging from 32.2 million Rubles in 1880 to 37.4 million Rubles in 1895. On the contrary, the national trade balance was considerably activated in 1886-1891 due to the measures taken by the then Minister of Finance Ivan A. Vyshnegradsky. The balance evolved from passive to active owing to boosted grain exports and imports contraction. By the mid-1890s the national gold reserve increased to the level of 873 million Rubles, partly because of the earlier loans conversion and making new loans in the European money market. The government was eventually able to accumulate a considerable gold reserve covering 87% of paper money in circulation.

Stabilization of the Ruble exchange rate against the gold parity placed it among the hardest currencies of the world. Since the reform of 1895-1897 and until the outbreak of the First World War the average value of the Russian Gold Ruble equaled 2.16 deutschemarks and 0.50 US dollar. Stable monetary and currency system contributed to rather high rates of economic growth, industrialization of the country, expansion of external economic relations. While sticking to the gold

---

9 Boris V. Annanich B.V., "Denezhnaya reforma 1895-1897 i vvedenie zolotogo standarta", *Istoriya Banka Rossii. 1860-2010*, Moscow, T. 1. S, p. 272-286.

standard Russia almost doubled its economic potential. The system of gold standard was abolished by Russia as well as by other European countries after the First World War had begun.

By the time the currency reform was initiated Russia's gold holdings had been enough to let Witte implement his plan. However, the Minister of Finance was apprehensive about the outflow of gold abroad, and that impelled him to put forward the initiative of founding a Russian reinsurance company. According to the law the State Bank was entitled to issue paper money unbacked by gold up to a figure of 300 million Rubles. The decline in the State Bank's gold reserves would challenge the successful implementation of the reform as such.

It should be taken into account that before the gold standard was adopted the empire's international account balance had constantly been negative, with the payments deficit amounting to one billion Rubles as has been estimated by an American economist Paul Gregory.

Table 1. Russia's international account balance, 1881-1897 (million Rubles)[10]

Exports surplus	+ 2,517
Interest payments on and redemptions of government loans	– 2,267
Foreign companies' dividends and income transferred abroad	– 415
Expenses made by the Russian tourists abroad	– 716
Other expenses	– 129
PAYMENTS DEFICIT	– 1,010

It is known that Witte stood in every possible way against the increment in deficit items of the balance of payments, and especially against the increase in expenses made by the Russian tourists abroad. The Finance Ministry officially encouraged Russian subjects to refrain from long journeys to the European countries, and particularly to France to attend the World Fair in Paris where Russians spent tens of millions Rubles. Witte's attention was also focused on the item "Other expenses" which recorded among other things the fire reinsurance incomes transferred abroad.

That was the reason why projecting the reform initiated in 1895, Witte envisaged in advance the control measures regulating the activities of Russian insurance companies and aimed at reducing the amount of gold transferred by such companies abroad. In 1894, a state insurance supervi-

10 Paul Gregory (1982), *Russian National Income, 1885-1913*, Cambridge, Cambridge University Press, p. 97-98.

sory body was set up with responsibility for the activities of the insurance companies, which at the same time were subject to mandatory reporting. The government fixed the size of joint-stock required to maintain every insurance transaction (500 thousand Rubles) and the incremental dividend rate (6% of the fixed capital) the company was entitled to pay unless the organization costs were paid off. The supervision over all the insurance companies was assigned to the Ministry of Interior (and that was the reason why in November 1894 Witte sent the above-mentioned letter to the Minister of Interior).

Apart from the Russian companies, there were three foreign joint-stock life insurance companies operating in the Russian market by the time: the New York Life (1885, US), the L'Urbaine (France, 1889) and the Equitable Life (US, 1889). They established their own subsidiaries and conducted insurance operations in the Russian internal market. All the above-mentioned companies specialized exclusively in providing personal insurance to private individuals[11]. Opening of foreign subsidiaries used to be a universal trend in the insurance business at that time, since "naturalized" companies succeeded in clearing the barriers of state protectionism (discriminatory regulation of activities), broadening its customer base and evading excessive taxation in the host country[12]. With appearance of foreign insurance companies in Russia's domestic market, the country became involved in the system of international economic relations which manifested itself in the explosive development of the reinsurance market. Nonetheless, the aforesaid three insurance companies, which transferred part of their income abroad, were not supposed to be included into the projected reinsurance society, since they were not engaged in fire insurance.

In parallel with regulation of the insurance business, preparations were made to adopt the gold standard. On February 4, 1895 the Minister of Finance presented the report to the emperor Nicolas II concerning the necessity to place the Russian ruble on the gold standard. It is fair to say that the reform started from the introduction of gold as an element of currency circulation. Gold transactions were allowed by the law of May 8, 1895. Under the law of May 24, 1895 every office and branch of the State Bank was empowered to buy gold coin, whilst some branches were permitted to make payments using such coin.

---

11 S. L. Efimov, V. V. Akimov, V. N. Borzyh (1997), *Strahovoe delo v Rossii: vehi istorii*, Moscow, Russkoe slovo.

12 Robin Pearson (2010), "Introduction: Towards an international History of Insurance", in Robin Pearson (ed.), *The Development of International Insurance*, London, Pickering and Chatto, p. 13.

Virtually at the same time, on May 30, 1895, the project of the foundation of the Russian Reinsurance Company was brought up for discussion to the Committee of Ministers, i.e. it was to be considered by a top-level governmental body. The presentations prepared by the Ministers of Finance and Interior stressed the evident impossibility to go without services provided by the foreign reinsurance business – the fact that had impelled the Russian government in 1866 to allow national companies to freely reinsure their business with foreign insurance companies. "But at present", the document stipulated, "when the number of joint-stock insurance companies alone has risen to thirteen, and the total sum insured with the aforesaid companies amounts to several billion Rubles, then the practice of reinsuring most risks with foreign companies is deemed quite detrimental and the establishment of the national insurance industry is welcome"[13].

"Taking care of searching out the measures to set up the national reinsurance business without direct government interference", the Minister of Finance suggested Russian insurance companies to be involved. Thus, the government initiative was disguised by creating the pool of private insurance companies. Those companies put forward the idea of establishing a new company and sharing part of their risks with it, proceeding from the premise that the new company's activity "will at least considerably diminish the yearly increasing outflow of the Russian companies' financial resources abroad, if not completely stop it".

In order to assess the project, it is useful to have a look at a brief excursus into the history of Russia's presence in the global fire reinsurance market. In 1851, Russian insurance companies received the initial permission to enter the global insurance market and conclude reinsurance contracts abroad partly retaining the risks, and in 1866 that operation was freed from any formal restrictions.

Reinsurance operations took two major organizational forms: mutual reinsurance by the insurance companies (the oldest form) and reinsurance through the specialist companies which emerged in the latter half of the 19th century. These companies came to play a leading role in the global reinsurance market, with the Munich-Re (German) and the Swiss-Re (Switzerland) taking the lead. The moment Russian companies became involved in the reinsurance business virtually coincided with an explosive development of that segment of the global insurance market[14].

---

13 RGIA. F. 1263. Op. 2. D. 5128. L. 482-486.

14 Robin Pearson (2010), "Introduction: Towards an international History of Insurance", in Robin Pearson (ed.), *The Development of International Insurance*, London, Pickering and Chatto, p. 12.

The first foreign companies to purchase insurance from Russian societies were of British origin, with the London insurance company "Phoenix" playing the most active role. On account of a gradual increase in competition between participants in the insurance market, the business was found unprofitable[15]. British companies were little by little leaving the Russian market due to high risks and severe losses they had suffered and were mainly replaced by German societies. By the late 19th century, Germany had taken the lead in the global insurance industry, however still lagging behind Great Britain and the USA by the volume of direct insurance operations. Until the 1880s, there was only the Magdeburg Fire Insurance Company operating in Russia whereas in the 1890s the Russian insurance market witnessed an enhanced inflow of German insurers. By the late 19th century, around 70 foreign companies were involved in Russia's fire reinsurance business. Among them the Munich-Re, the Cologne-Re, and the Swiss-Re (Zurich) were the largest reinsurance companies.

All the Russian companies largely involved in insurance undertook reinsurance business as well, although they did it on a far smaller scale than the international companies did. The attempts were made to get the Russian reinsurance industry going with a view to get rid of the payments in favor of foreign reinsurers. In 1889, the All-Russian Reinsurance Society was even announced to have been set up, however the project remained ink on paper because of the insurance companies' fears of confiding their insurance business to a new institution[16]. In 1892, the declaration was made concerning the establishment of a new society under the same name, but that company also failed to start operations. In such a way, Witte's initiative was the third attempt to finally arrange mutual reinsurance industry in Russia and reduce foreign payments in the form of reinsurance premium.

Justifying his project of the Russian Reinsurance Society Witte put forward the meaningful data on the dynamics of Russia's fire reinsurance business.

---

15 Y. A. Feygin (1915), "Perestrakhovanie, ego istoriya i sovremennoe polozhenie". (Reinsurance, its history and the contemporary situation), *Strakhovoe obozrenie.* 10. (An overview of insurance), n.10. s. 696-697.

16 Poyasnitel'naya zapiska k proektu uchrezhdeniya v Rossii obschestva peresrakhovaniya (Explanatory note on the proposed establishment of a general reinsurance company). St Petersburg 1887; Ustav Vserossiyskogo obschestva peresrakhovaniya, uchrezhdennogo v 1889 (Articles of Association of the All-Russian Reinsurance Company establish in 1889). St Petersburg 1889.

Table 2. Data on fire insurance operations undertaken by Russian joint-stock insurance societies during 1827-1890, thousand Rubles[17]

Year	Insured sum	Premium income			Fire losses		
		Total	Transferred to reinsurers	Accumulated by insurers	Total	Covered by reinsurers	Covered by insurers
1827-1850	3,084,471.5	19,558.0	0	19,558.0	8,742.7	0	8,742.7
1860	741,116.7	4,510.9	1,072.7	3,438.2	3,569.4	666.1	2,903.3
1870	1,302,924.0	8,446.9	4,802.2	3,644.7	4,497.0	2,803.5	1,693.5
1880	3,983,857.1	25,759.1	16,929.9	8,829.3	18,816.2	13,201.4	5,614.7
1890	4,823,585.2	31,204.6	18,567.8	12,636.8	22,919.9	13,459.1	9,460.7

As Table 2 shows, the fire insurance operations started expanding rapidly in the 1860s (apparently, owing to the fact that Russian insurance companies were officially permitted to reinsure their risks with foreign companies without any restrictions). Already by 1870, the bulk of the total premium income had come to be transferred to foreign reinsurers if compared to the premium income accumulated by Russian insurers, and by 1890 that gap had almost doubled amounting to 31.2 and 18.6 million Rubles respectively. However, the data on fire losses presents a slightly different picture: from 1880 to 1890 the fire losses covered by reinsurers remained basically at the same level (around 13 million Rubles, whereas the fire losses covered by insurers nearly doubled (from 5.6 to 9.5 million Rubles).

According to the information of the Finance Ministry, for thirty years (1851-1882) the Russian insurance companies had collected premiums to the value of 332.4 million Rubles of which 185.1 million Rubles were transferred to foreign companies and 147.3 million Rubles accumulated by the Russian societies. As a matter of interest, foreign reinsurers lost on the whole 2.2 million Rubles during the period under review, whereas Russian societies earned the income amounting to 13.5 million Rubles. When a wave of fires swept across the country in 1882 a milestone was passed. Foreign companies had to spent all their premiums reaching 21 million Rubles for insurance compensation plus 7 million Rubles from their internal funds, while the Russian companies' loss was equal to around 1.5 million Rubles. From 1883 on, Russian companies were raising tariffs, began assessing risks more accurately, and the fire insurance regained its profitability. In 1883-1893 the total premiums amounted to 359 million

[17] Ob uchrezhdenii Obschestva Russkogo perestrakhovaniya. Slushano v Komitete ministrov 30 maya 1895 g. RGIA. F. 1263. Op. 2. D. 5128. L. 482-505 verso.

Rubles including 134 million Rubles yielded by Russian and 225 million Rubles – by foreign companies. Out of total 48 million Rubles earned as the net income 13 million Rubles accounted for Russian and 35 million Rubles – for foreign insurers.

In the meantime in line with the established practice, foreign companies reinsured large Russian objects (factories, depot etc.) which valued at several million Rubles and were unable to be insured by a single company because of excessively high risks. According to expert evaluations, 80-90% of the insured value of those risks was annually accepted by foreign reinsurers, and such operations did not inflict losses on them: in 1883-1893 foreign reinsurers earned an average income (calculated as the ratio of the net premium to the gross-premium amounting to 15.5%, whereas for Russian societies dealing with less valuable real property this figure was 10%.

According to Witte in 1891-1893 out of a total income of 99 million Rubles 53.2 million Rubles (or 54%) were transferred abroad – the fact that was fraught with consequences to Russia's balance of payments. In the meantime only 6-7% of the total premiums collected by Russian companies were reinsured within the country. "Since the 1880s, more specifically since 1883", Witte emphasized, "this operation has been seriously damaging our international balance of payments due to nonrefundable losses caused by transferring considerable sums abroad".

As was later argued by the governmental authorities, "the reinsurance operation undertaken by Russian insurance societies was characterized by the lopsided development and involved mainly transferring own risks to foreign companies without accepting for reinsurance sufficient insured value from them and without conducting reinsurance business between Russian societies at an adequate level". By the moment the Russian Reinsurance Society was set up the situation had not changed yet. In 1895 out of the total premium of 39.3 million Rubles collected by Russian fire insurance societies only 2.5 million Rubles (or some 6.5%) resulted from domestic reinsurance operations, whereas 24.1 million Rubles (or 65%) were transferred to foreign reinsurers[18].

Apart from inflicting nonrefundable losses in the form of foreign companies' net income, making business with foreign reinsurers, as Witte stressed, "leads to a temporary, but a tremendous capital outflow from the country in the form of premiums transferred abroad which totaled 15 million Rubles in 1891-1893. The premium collection falls on the winter months, i.e. on the period our exports slacken and the capital outflow reaches its peak".

[18] *Ibid.* F. 23. Op. 24. D. 234. L. 96-100.

To sum up, as the Minister of Finance concluded his report presented to the Committee of Ministers, "having no solid ground within the empire Russian societies make themselves completely dependent upon foreign companies which do not hesitate to dictate terms to Russian societies as it happened in 1882, otherwise threatening a full rupture of relations. It has happened several times that foreign companies' refused to bear the fire loss in case fire accidents were becoming more frequent, and Russian societies are not secured from that to happen again in the future"[19].

Witte was planning to persuade the cofounders of the projected Russian Reinsurance Company to assume responsibilities to reinsure abroad only a certain rate of their excess (25%), i.e. the risk portion they were going to rid of, with the rest being transferred to a new company (25%) and reinsured between each other (50%). According to Witte's estimates, foreign companies would eventually collect 21% of the total premium income instead of 54% they received de facto in 1891-1893 that was supposed to let Russian societies increase their own share in accepted risks and at the same time diminish the sums transferred abroad"[20].

Referring to the international practices, Witte reminded that mutual reinsurance was highly developed in Western Europe. In particular he introduced an example that German insurance companies earned around one third of their income by accepting reinsurance on each other, whereas in Russia that rate hardly equaled to 6% of the total premium income. "If instead of developing mutual reinsurance", the project initiator insisted, "we will hope for further involvement of foreign reinsurers, then Russian societies are at risk of turning into mere commission agents controlled by western companies. Here lies the danger of practice established by us and residing in underwriting our own risks in favor of foreign insurance companies without accepting reinsurance from them"[21].

Not only foreign reinsurance did no harm, as Witte explained, but was it able to make a positive contribution if mutual risk acceptance is set up, and such a system had long been in existence in Western Europe. A similar trend was in evidence in the Russian empire: specifically, since the 1890s the insurance company "Rossiya" had begun establishing its foreign branches in order to accept fire reinsurance from foreign partners. However, the above-mentioned operation was fairly characterized by Witte as being "in the embryonic state". Indeed, Russian companies made their

---

19 *Ibid.* F. 1263. Op. 2. D. 5128. L. 491-492.

20 *Ibid.* L. 493.

21 Po voprosu ob uchrezhdenii Obschestva Russkogo perestrakhovaniya. Slushano v Komitete ministrov 30 maya 1895 g. *Ibid.* L. 528-539.

massive entrance into the international foreign insurance market later – at the early 20th century[22].

Witte precipitated the foundation of the Russian Reinsurance Society so much that he moved on without awaiting the insurance companies' formal decisions approved by their shareholders' general meetings. Instead, he reached a direct agreement with the management of twelve insurance companies who consented to become the co-founders of a newly established company providing three out of six million Rubles of its basic capital and to set up a special Council to which one representative from every co-founder was appointed. The minister was convinced that "playing a decisive role in eliminating the dependence of the Russian insurance business from foreign insurance companies and in putting an end to the transfer of national savings abroad, the domestic reinsurance will also encourage the decrease in insurance premiums and the rapid emergence of new insurance companies"[23].

On June 9, 1895, i.e. a week later after the project's consideration by the Committee of Ministers, the company's charter was approved by the emperor. The main task stipulated by the document was as follows: "The society is entitled to accept various reinsurance from Russian and foreign insurance companies and institutions as well as reinsure the risks accepted by itself from other insurance societies both Russian and foreign"[24].

However, from the very beginning Witte's undertaking came across the resistance of foreign reinsurers. The attempts by the Russian companies to make contracts on new terms were met with a refusal as long as the reduced volume of reinsurance did not offer prospects of sufficiently high income. Having no intention to rupture the relations with foreign partners, especially in a situation when Russian societies were eager to open their branches abroad, Russian companies raised the percentage of the foreign companies' excess from 25% to 45%, of which Witte himself got to know "by accident"[25].

In the end, the Company underwrote 40% of its risks with foreign reinsurers while accepting 36% for its own account and spreading the rest of 24% among Russian companies (by 2% for every of the twelve parent companies). Thus, the system was designed entailing both domestic and external (foreign) reinsurance. The interests of policyholders remained intact as long as the size of premium was not changed.

22 Yury A. Petrov (2012), "Russia: Early expansion, state involvement, and re-emergence of the insurance industry", in Borscheid and Haueter (eds.), *World Insurance. The Evolution of a Global Risk Network*, Oxford, Oxford University Press, p. 213-238.

23 RGIA. F. 1263. Op. 2. D. 5128. L. 539.

24 Ustav Obschestva Russkogo perestrakhovaniya. SPb., 1895. S. 1.

25 RGIA. F. 1263. Op. 2. D. 5128. L. 528.

However, the Russian Reinsurance Company failed to reduce the proportion of foreign reinsurance in the Russian reinsurance industry. At first it was doing all right: it was even ranked among the leaders of the European reinsurance market by the total premium income. In 1896, the company collected premiums to the value of 7.2 million Rubles, in 1897 – 8.1 million Rubles, whereas apart from the Munich-Re whose total premium income in 1897 amounted to 45.2 deutschemarks (around 20 million Rubles) there were no more German or Austro-Hungarian companies that could boast such results. Witte had assigned the task to curtail the outflow of gold from the country, which was used for settlements with foreign reinsurers. Although that task was not completed, the Russian gold reserves were not seriously endangered forasmuch as the currency reform was successfully accomplished in 1897. The Minister of Finance lost interest in the insurance business because of his failure to influence the level of payouts made by Russian companies in favor of their foreign partners.

Meanwhile the situation was changing under the influence of economic conditions. The economic crisis of the late 19th – early 20th centuries entailed a profitability decline for Russian fire insurance companies impelling all Russian insurance companies to accept more reinsurance from abroad. The leading companies began opening their foreign branches in order to carry out insurance and reinsurance operations abroad, and that made them less interested in a Russian corporate body. That resulted in a considerable decline in the rate of premiums transferred by the Russian fire insurance companies to the foreign insurers in relation to the gross premium written: 51.5% in 1898 against 65% in 1895. In the meantime the direct mutual reinsurance between Russian societies experienced a rapid upsurge, with its rate rising from 6.5% in 1895 to 21.5% in 1898. Eventually the total premium income earned by the Russian Reinsurance Company fell down the level of only 5.8 million Rubles[26].

Referring to a substantial fire loss suffered in 1896-1897, the Company's co-founders lowered the rate of their excess from the initial 50% level to 20%[27], and in 1900 the basic capital was reduced from six to three million Rubles. "The capital reduction to three million Rubles", the leaders of the Russian insurance market emphasized, "should have no impact on the company's prominent position among Russian and especially foreign insurance companies by the size of its basic capital". In Russia there were only two companies whose capitals exceeded the level of three million Rubles – the Russian Reinsurance Company and the "Rossiya" (each companies' capital equaled to four million Rubles). In

26 *Ibid.* F. 23. Op. 24. D. 234. L. 96-100.

27 *Ibid.* L. 69-70.

Germany the capital of the Munich Reinsurance Company amounted to only 2.5 million deutschemarks, i.e. around one million Rubles[28]. However, such statements were nothing more than an attempt to put a brave face of a sorry business.

The economic crisis entailed severe problems. If in 1899 the Company closed a fiscal year with a small income of 134 thousand Rubles, the following year was ended with a loss of 280 thousand Rubles[29]. In 1903, the Company earned 465 thousand Rubles income without experiencing any loss in the years that followed. However, contrary to the expectations of its co-founders, the company did not play a prominent part in the reinsurance market.

In 1906, in line with the other Russian companies operating in the USA insurance marker, the Company's management deposited the 500 thousand dollars (one million Rubles) pledge to undertake reinsurance operations in the USA with a view to covering that capital outflow from Russia by a newly generated income[30]. Nevertheless, the Russian Reinsurance Company later invested almost all of its funds into highly liquid assets: in 1913, out of the total company's income of 526.1 thousand Rubles the interest income on securities amounted to 307 thousand Rubles including 202 thousand Rubles gained from the Russian securities (the government bonds and the railroad and land banks securities pledged by the state) and 105 thousand Rubles the foreign securities yielded, mainly the bonds issued by the city of New York and District Columbia. In such a way, the three-fifths of the Company's income came from the rent-seeking investments in securities. Insurance and reinsurance operations as such appeared to be marginal in terms of its earning power.

Cherishing the idea of a mutual insurance company in the mid-1890s, Witte accused the then Russian insurance companies of "an excessive timorousness" for as long as instead of being actively engaged in the insurance market activities, they preferred receiving a small, though a sure income from investing their huge capitals accumulated over past years in interest bearing securities"[31]. To be sure, Witte's creation failed to move beyond the Russian patriarchal model where companies gave precedence to a small, though a sure income over highly remunerative risks, and to making business directly with the global insurance market participants over getting involved in the activities of the national corporate mutual insurance body.

28 *Ibid.* L. 96-100.

29 Otchet Obschestva Russkogo perestrakhovaniya za 1899 god. SPb., 1900; To zhe za 1900 god. SPb., 1901.

30 RGIA. F. 23. Op. 24. D. 234. L. 170-171.

31 *Ibid.* F. 1263. Op. 2. D. 5128. L. 535.

International Reinsurance in the 1920s

André Straus

On the eve of the First World War, the worldwide reinsurance landscape was dominated by only a few actors. Germany was the leader, while Austria-Hungary and Russia occupied the second rank. Finally, two Bulgarian companies practised pure reinsurance at international level. However, the reinsurance industry could still be found in Swiss and Scandinavian countries. In France and in Belgium, besides some professional reinsurers, the primary insurance companies also ran the reinsurance branch. Notably, reinsurance in Britain and North America was virtually non-existent. The reinsurance system adopted in England involved the mutual sharing of risks with other primary insurers (coinsurance). According to Gerathewohl, in the middle of the 19th century this approach was adopted in other countries, including the United States. There, reinsurance practice and reinsurance companies were slow to develop, due partly to legal restrictions.[1] From a historical point of view, two facts appear astonishing. Britain was the first country which developed the practice of insurance on a large scale, but nevertheless British reinsurance remained weak for a very long **time**. On the other hand, the United States, in becoming the first economic power in the world, was probably that country where the value of things susceptible to insurance was the highest; however, the development of professional reinsurance was unknown there. This double statement raises the crucial question of the relationship between insurance and reinsurance. Some initial answers could be put forward to explain the lack of professional reinsurance in Anglo-Saxon countries. In this chapter, I ask, first, to what extent reinsurance was essential for the sound working of insurance. Secondly, I ask to what extent the organizational structure of the pure reinsurance companies was necessary in order for them to play the roles they are playing, comparatively speaking, with coinsurance; and finally, I ask whether the necessity for professional reinsurance was or was not dependent on the branches which insurance companies used to run. Probably, neither hypothesis excludes other explanations.

1 Klaus Gerathewohl (1982), *Reinsurance Principles and Practice*. Trans. John Christopher La Bonté. Vol. II. Karlsruhe: Verlag Versicherungswirtschaft e. V., p. 693.

We have to offer more precision regarding the first stages of reinsurance development. This development was a consequence of economic, industrial and technological development. In Britain, very early progress in insurance came with the marine insurance. In continental Europe, the real setting up of professional reinsurance activities accompanied fire insurance, which grew very quickly during the 19th century. In the United States, certainly, the very first reinsurance activities were connected with life insurance.

There is no consensus among scholars regarding the eventual effect of the First World War on the reinsurance industry. For Peter Borscheid,[2] unlike insurance, the network of which had been patiently built up during the last decades of the 19th century, but which broke down and was not able to recover until after Second World War, reinsurance succeeded in partially repairing the breaches between the insurance markets, heavily affected by the War. Nevertheless, Borscheid entitles his chapter "Breaking Point – The First World War". In the same book, David Gugerli claims that "except for in Germany, the First World War did not represent such a watershed in the history of reinsurance. The 54th annual report of the board of directors of Swiss Re, reporting on the 1917 business year, barely even mentioned the war."[3] But besides the statement that "for the industry as a whole, there was no dramatic change",[4] others scholars could describe the war period and the two decades that follow as "The Thirty Years War (1914 – 1945)".[5] They are referring to the two World Wars and to the Great Crash of 1929.

Four main topics could be envisaged as being important during this period. Firstly, there was a shift among reinsurers as a consequence of the conflict, and of the Russian revolution. Secondly, due partly to the dismemberment of the Central Empires and the withdrawal of Russia from the world market (and therefore for many insurers, and the new countries appearing on the scene, a change of reinsuring partners), the role of the new states backed up the setting of a new reinsurance industry. The third point is the geographical expansion of the reinsurance industry, which

---

2 Peter Borscheid (2013), "Global Insurance Networks", in Harold James, Peter Borscheid, David Gugerli, and Tobias Strauman, *The Value of Risk. Swiss Re and the History of Reinsurance*, Oxford, Oxford University Press, p. 70.

3 David Gugerli (2013), "Cooperation and Competition Organization and Risk in The Reinsurance Business 1860–2010", in Harold James, Peter Borscheid, David Gugerli and Tobias Strauman, *The Value of Risk. Swiss Re and the History of Reinsurance*, p. 175. Peter Borscheid (2013), "Global Insurance Networks", in Harold James, Peter Borscheid, David Gugerli and Tobias Strauman, *The Value of Risk. Swiss Re and the History of Reinsurance*, Oxford, Oxford University Press, p. 70.

4 *Idem.*

5 Henri Leblanc (1949), *La réassurance du point de vue économique*, Paris, L.G.D.J., p. 149.

accompanied the extension of primary insurers. Finally, the ongoing new development of industrialization led to the birth of new risks, some of them bearing the possibility of huge damages, encouraging the development both of insurance and of news technics about reinsurance.

We can confirm, first of all, that the First World War did cause a severe shift in market shares among reinsurers. Among the three leaders on the eve of the War, two virtually disappeared as protagonists, Germany and Russia. Others countries which knew reinsurance practice and had begun a certain development of it before the War took advantage of the semi-retirement of Germany and Russia. There were, at first, the countries that stayed neutral during the War. This was the case with Scandinavian countries like Denmark, Norway and Sweden. As Germany was defeated and the three Central Empires were sliced up, the political frame of the European space underwent huge changes.

A second explanation for the expanding activities of the reinsurance industry after the Second World War was the wide changes in the political frame of the European space following the First World War. From a political and cultural point of view, the period stemming from the Great War was characterized by patriotism and more nationalistic feeling at most levels of society.

Germany

Of all the effects of the War on German reinsurance, the most impacted branch was fire reinsurance, the main markets for which were the United States, England and France. Consequently, the volume of acceptances collected fell at the beginning of the War. By contrast, the German reinsurance of life insurance, the main market for which was Austria-Hungary, was able to maintain its position until the dismemberment of the Empire. But the worst hit to both German insurance and reinsurance was the fall of the mark and the excessively large inflation suffered as a result. The direct consequence for reinsurance was a rocketing amount of cessions, which hit not only the ancient companies, which could then compensate for the loss of their foreign markets, but a multiplicity of new societies (192 in 1922 and 1923) which disappeared as quickly as they had been launched. In addition, the first thing it was necessary to do was to rebuild the national insurance industry.

The result of this crisis was the reinforcement of the old companies, mainly the strongest such as Munich Re, which could absorb a great number of portfolios. Thus, the concentration movement around reinsurance, which had begun around 1880, could continue after the War. From a financial point of view, it is interesting to notice the development of the compulsory quota-share treaty, which shows the desire of the new or rebuilt primary companies to be backed by reinsurers. The strong recovery of German reinsurance is clearly demonstrated by the growth in the amount of gross premiums collected by Munich Re from 1924 until the end of the 1920s.

Year	Marks	Year	Marks
1913	200	*1921*	1,100
1914	204	*1922*	2,016
1915	177	*1923*	867,686
1916	194	*1924*	65
1917	193	*1925*	127
1918	254	*1926*	137
1919	367	*1927*	154
1920	508	*1928*	285

The others German reinsurers underwent a similar evolution. We have to notice that the risks, which suffered the most, were fire and transport. By contrast, life insurance and casualty insurance regained their pre-war numbers. As early as 1926 Munich Re was active again in the French market, and on the eve of the crisis it had attained a position better than it had enjoyed before the War.

But if German reinsurance recovered in volume the business it had had before, its quality was lower. The most profitable markets of the former period, such as fire insurance in the United States, had been replaced by lower quality risks. In order to compensate for the big reduction in fire reinsurance, German reinsurers had developed their acceptances in transport, in casualty, and in some branches where return was less profitable (as in credit reinsurance). The case of transport is particularly interesting. During the War, reinsurers had been excluded from the market, to the benefit of British reinsurers. When, from 1924 onwards, they tried to recover their business relationships, they met for the first time with easy success, which was attributed by the German press to their technical skills and to their strong reputation. This view is not completely wrong, but study of the accounts of the British and of the Scandinavian societies furnishes a further explanation. From the War onwards, the results of the maritime businesses were so catastrophic that British brokers were happy to find societies accepting at the same price business that British companies were more and more reluctant to accept without changing the premiums.

Two more reasons may explain why the quality of business for German reinsurers was not as good as expected. The first is over-concurrence, which led to a drop in tariffs and an increase in the acquisition cost, which can be seen in the evolution of the loss ratio. The harm coming from the primary companies spread to reinsurance, with an even worse effect because the ceding insurers began to unload onto reinsurers the bad or underrated risks they had accepted too easily. At that time, there was another general claim against primary companies. They were accused of having used reinsurance with the sole aim of increasing the number of their clients, without sufficient precautions.

In the other countries the situation was identical, showing the same symptoms, most of time at a lower degree: a wave of new companies being launched which disappeared as quickly as they had appeared, and mergers and acquisitions in the older companies, following a trend present before the War. In all sizeable countries, the questions then posed were, firstly, to rebuild a national insurance and reinsurance industry, and secondly to re-create an international net.

Evidently, the common feature of that evolution was that some countries among the Allied, neutral or new countries appearing as a result of the peace treaties took the place of Germany in the new Europe. The fight was particularly stark with regard to the truncated Austria-Hungary. The two biggest companies in primary insurance in terms of their reinsurance portfolios (Riunione Adriatica and Assicurazioni Generali) became Italian when the Trenten did. The Erste Bömische Rückversicherungsbank fell to Czechoslovakia. Austria kept the Wiener Rück, and Hungry the Budapest and the Pannonia. The Budapest Reinsurance company was founded in 1911 as a subsidiary of the Gazdak, the insurance company representing farming interests in Hungary. Germany had to undergo reconstruction since the explosive inflation of 1923 had wreaked havoc. This left Italy and the powerful companies of Trieste to invest in Austrian and Danube insurance. Italy was not alone in trying to gain market share in these new markets. France, with the Compagnie française de réassurance, Switzerland with Swiss Re in Romania and Yugoslavia, Denmark in Austria and Hungary challenged Germany fiercely. The result was that all the companies at that time pronounced the unfavourable results of their acceptances in those areas.

Another important section of the reinsurance business in which German reinsurers had problems of their own was that of accident, third-party and motor reinsurance. Germany was pressing ahead for the motorization of the population, and, notwithstanding government safeguarding measures, the increasing traffic intensity had led to an increase in accident frequency, which necessarily adversely affected reinsurance business.

The exceptional position the Munich Reinsurance Company occupied always put that company in a class by itself. The two large sectors of the German reinsurance market were the professional reinsurance companies, of which there were twenty, and the direct–indirect writing companies, including the Allianz Stuttgarter Verein, and the Aachener and Münchener Feuer, which, like their opposite partners abroad, were interested in reinsurance on a not-little scale.

Italy

In the other branches of reinsurance the situation was similar. In life, German reinsurers were replaced, in large measure, by Italian ones. Italy was then the big beneficiary of the dismembered Austro-Hungarian State. Italian reinsurance was quite insignificant before the War and was in large part dependent on foreign companies, but in 1927 it attained world importance. The leading firms were Unione Italiana, founded in 1922, Assicurazioni Generali (with their subsidiaries Compania Riunita di Sicurità and Compania Generali di Assicurazioni) and Assicuratrice italiana, which had absorbed the Riassicuratrice, itself founded by Riunione Adriatica.

The former Austrian companies had been developed so far during the War that the Italian reinsurance industry became an exporter.

In million liras		
	Cessions	**Acceptances**
Fire		
– Pure reinsurers	110	190
– Other Companies	200	140
Transport		
– Pure reinsurers	100	130
– Other Companies	300	100

In life, Italian companies were compulsorily reinsured by Unione Italiana. This branch grew considerably during the War, since the cessions' total did not reach 5 million lire before the War, and reached almost 50 million lire in 1926.

Russia

Russia, which was also a major player in international reinsurance, also disappeared from the international market. In a first stage, Russian foreign business had grown very quickly. In the United States, Russian companies, which had collected 16 million dollars in 1913, collected 26 million dollars of premiums in 1917. When the Revolution broke up, some companies shifted their activities to foreign countries. In 1918, the Rossia and the Salamandra founded subsidiaries in Denmark. Those close to the boundaries had an advantage. This may explain why this transfer was realized by companies from Petrograd and not by those from Moscow.

The problem faced by the Russian subsidiaries launched in the United States was different. As the US government did not recognize the new Russian authorities, these firms were without nationality. Most of them were liquidated between 1920 and 1923, and the Federal Office of Insurance managed their assets. Only the subsidiaries of the Salamandra and the Rossia could subsist. The business of the first was transferred to the Danish subsidiary, and an American company was launched under the name of Rossia of America to exploit the portfolio of the Rossia. In 1926, the Rossia of America was the third-largest pure reinsurance company in the world.

In Russia, the reinsurance gained control by means of a monopoly, Gosstrach, which operated as the reinsurer of three primary mutual companies besides itself. For the fire branch only, the indirect remittances of Gosstrach increased from 400,000 roubles in 1923 to 2,300,000 roubles in 1926. From a macroeconomic point of view, this means that post in the balance of account of Russia had become in deficit. The task of Witte was destroyed.

From an international point of view, Russia practically disappeared for a time, both as a purveyor and a customer of reinsurance. The result was a reduction of the supply of reinsurance, which benefited Denmark first, then the states which had split from the Soviet Union.

Denmark

In Denmark, the situation had changed, not only because the two former Russian companies were going to occupy the first rank, but also because the absence of Germany and Russia benefited the ancient companies (Skandinavia, Nordisk) as well.

In 1903, the Danish professional reinsurers collected, in fire, only 15 million crowns; for the whole branches, in 1923, they collected 190 million crowns (the primary insurers collected 146 million in reinsurance). The founding of an American firm reduced that total to 227 million in 1926. Nonetheless, with 135 million of cessions Denmark kept its export position, in second place just behind Switzerland, which it even exceeded in transport. It is noticeable that transport was particularly developed in the first post-war period, both in Demark and in the other Scandinavian countries. In Denmark alone, a hundred or so insurance or reinsurance companies were launched in the maritime business. Most of these disappeared within a few years.

Besides their favourable geographical situation, this boom can be explained by their neutrality, and in fact, the Allies ceded to the three countries (Denmark, Norway and Sweden) a large share of their maritime excess. Their acceptances increased, from 24 million crowns in 1913 to more than 520 million in 1920. But this situation was exceptional and due to the War. With the disappearance of those exceptional circumstances, the Scandinavian countries knew a sudden fall. The acceptances dropped from 520 million crowns in 1920 to 165 in 1923 and 108 in 1927.

If the marine branch was the first to suffer from an exaggerated demand caused by the War, the behaviour of the other branches followed, albeit later.

Finland and Poland

In these two states, which had separated from Russia, the situation was quite like that of the successors of the former Austria-Hungary. On the basis of what had been a part of the former great Russian reinsurance industry, Finland developed a national industry (which was necessary, due to the gravity of the risks: forests, the timber industry); the Finnish fire insurance needed a great retrocession. In 1912, the amount of acceptances was 3 million Finnish marks, in 1920 12 million, and in 1926 36 million for the professional reinsurers and 44 million for the other companies.

In Poland, a pure reinsurance company was launched in 1920. The *Warta* collected, in 1927, around 14 million zlotys.

Switzerland

Contrary to Denmark, the other great beneficiary of the weakness of Germany, Switzerland, continued in a regular form the growth which had begun before the War. The Swiss Re took the place of the Munich Re in the markets of the victor countries.

Years	Swiss Re Swiss francs	Munich Re Marks
1910	35,634,784	166,631,730
1911	42,954,466	176,320,852
1812	47,571,413	189,493,219
1913	51,677,607	199,605,003
1914	55,935,064	204,454,297
1915	63,968,025	176,893,080
1916	80,018,306	199,417,288
1917	101,192,909	192,757,611
1918	126,200,139	253,808,558
1919	140,785,316	366,688,975
1920	174,690,316	508,170,262
1921	158,456,663	1,100,206,191
1922	157,944,184	2,016,062,547
1923	181,947,386	86,786,430,613
1924	208,089,307	64,816,599
1925	236,919,870	1,265,261,188

Swiss Re, founded in Zurich in 1863, underwent very cautious growth. In 1875 it launched a branch, Prudentia, whose main goal was to play the role of retrocession to Swiss Re. A second company was created in 1918, the Zurich General Company (reinsurance). In 1914, Swiss Re was an important firm, with a solid basis and an ability to inspire truth. Then, it experienced fast growth, especially in the international field. It is noteworthy that Swiss Re, born from the primary Swiss insurance, was in its turn a precious help to its international development.

In 1924, the first year of stability in Germany, the pre-war situation was reversed, not only in terms of the comparison of the gross premiums, but also because foreign customers had changed their partners. Thus Swiss reinsurance, which had an excess in exports before the War of around 20 million in fire, increased its business in that branch to 120 million in

1927. In 1913, Swiss Re had extended its operations in the United States, where Munich Re had already been operating for a long time. At the end of the War its subsidiary, the Prudentia, had also been set up in the United States. The result was that, together, their business exceeded 12 million in 1926. This conquest of the Allied markets was indeed facilitated by the international position the Swiss insurance industry had already occupied before the War, but it can also be explained by the disappearance from the market of the German companies, inscribed on the "black list".

The neutrality and the strength of the Swiss franc gave a particular advantage to the Swiss in life reinsurance: for professional reinsurers, acceptances were multiplied by five between 1913 and 1927. Nevertheless, it was in casualties' reinsurance that the development was the greatest. Since the disarray of Germany did not benefit the growth of casualties and legal liability insurance, Swiss reinsurance saw the amount of its acceptances grow from 12 to 85 million. The outstanding growth of this branch was due in large part to the activity of the primary companies, which had conquered the European market and were working even in overseas countries.

The major characteristic of the Swiss reinsurance growth was its regularity. Despite a small crisis in 1921, in all branches, even in transport, the primes collected in 1927 exceeded those collected in 1920. In no other country was the development of reinsurance so continuous. This could be explained not only by the exceptional circumstances of the War and the following years, but also by the excellent standard of the control and the cautious behaviour of the reinsurers' managers. It is noticeable that during this period no setting up or failure of no viable companies were to deplore, as was the case in all other countries, even France and England.

Swiss professional reinsurance (1913–1927).
Gross premium (million Swiss francs)

Years	Fire	Transport	Life	Casualties	Others
1913	24.80	2.91	17.90	27.23	1.31
1920	155.26	15.45	47.07	67.43	
1927	252.97	27.99	64.98	81.06	36.09

The United Kingdom

In the United Kingdom, the professional reinsurance companies had failed to reach a state of solid existence before the First World War. Most of them perished very soon after being launched, and the few remaining ones (except for three) which had existed before the War vanished between 1914 and 1922. The oldest, the Mercantile and General, began in 1907; the other companies, which had been launched before 1907, were unable to develop and disappeared. Perhaps the main reason for the weaknesses of British reinsurance lay in the strength of the primary British companies, which devoted all their attention to direct production, leaving on the sidelines the relatively minor interest of reinsurance activity. Gobert adds the reluctance of the British vis-à-vis a system which was said to give to the concurrence too much information about their business and their clients.[6] Furthermore, the companies disliked the practice of reciprocity. After the War, there was a speedy increase in the number of new reinsurance companies: for example, eight sprang up in London in 1919. But the market reacted sharply: in 1924–6 the oldest companies themselves experienced difficulties. The two most important of these (City Equitable and Consolidated) felt bankruptcy. A further explanation for the lack of tradition and interest can be seen in the closing off of the European markets, where other countries, such as Denmark, Switzerland or Italy, were best placed to gather up the inheritance of German reinsurance. The British reinsurers had to search other markets, in America or the Far East (the Dominions, China). Thirdly, as for the Scandinavian countries, reinsurance transport was an important factor in the disappearance of the new British societies. Thorin[7] speaks of this branch of reinsurance as the "tonneau des Danaïdes"[8] for the companies.

Years	**Net premium**	**Claim paid**	**Underwriting reserves**
1921	579	687	369
1922	400	551	290
1923	422	399	320
1924	755	768	616
1925	590	833	614

France

In the first half of the 1920s, circumstances were more or less similar in France and in England. But France could more easily overcome the post-

6 Joseph Gobert (1923), *Étude sur la réassurance, ses avantages, ses dangers et son importance économique*, Bruxelles, A. de Reume.

7 Thorin (1929), *La réassurance contre l'incendie*, Orléans, Impr. Orleanaise.

8 A bottomless barrel.

war crisis. This was, firstly, because there existed in the pre-war period an autonomous professional reinsurance industry; and secondly, because the transport business constituted only a small part of the reinsurer's portfolios, which were more focused, as in Switzerland, on fire and casualties. The effort, which had in reality begun in 1914 to develop an independent French reinsurance industry, resulted in 1923, in an excess of exported premiums over imported ones. The French reinsurers worked essentially in foreign markets, especially in Great Britain where sixteen of them had sales representation. Despite the lack of precise statistics, according to La Réassurance we can give the following figures.

Years	**Gross premium**	**Retrocessions**	**Loss ratio**	**Total reserves**
1917	55,598	3,779	50.67	42,282
1920	144,605	28,698	52.86	87,684
1922	252,061	80,539	58.35	121,262
1924	421,266	165,409	58.23	193,195
1925	614,355	249,704	60.15	283,850
1926	697,473	303,765	61.12	317,305

According to Hollitscher, one can draw the following table for 1927.

	Cessions	**Acceptances**
Insurance companies, fire, casualties, hail, various branches	635	
Transport insurance companies: 40% of gross premiums	17	
Insurance companies against livestock mortality	5	
Retrocessions of reinsurance companies	368	
Insurance companies exploiting various branches without precisions: 40% of gross premiums		
Reinsurance companies		789
Endowment insurance companies in which only a third of the production is divided into direct and indirect business		283
Reinsurance companies against hail damages		18

Even though the information it presents is somewhat approximate, this table provides a relatively representative picture of the French reinsurance market in 1927. It was self-sufficient, and was becoming an exporter.

The pooling of the economic resources of the British and French empires was at the same time an indication of the firm determination to win the War, and of close collaboration and confidence that had marked Anglo-French relations. The joint action in world markets for essential goods made for greater stability and thus helped the two governments to keep inflationary movements to a minimum.

Outside Europe, this movement towards a national reinsurance industry spread through all countries. The United States erected harsh regulations, and, in setting up a "black list", hampered the activities of foreign reinsurers. National companies were founded, some of them with the portfolios of companies that were formerly foreign (for example: The Pilot, from the Munich; the Rossia, from the Danish Rossia; the North Star, from the Salamandra; and the Prudential, from the British Prudential). However, the primary companies remained the most important underwriters (according to Hollitscher, their acceptances soared from around 30 million in 1912 to 280 million in 1927).

In the turbulent history of reinsurance, the period between 1927 and 1933 had been relatively peaceful. The main feature from then onwards up until after the Second World War was the setting up of national markets, often under the control of the State. For the first time, private reinsurance, and then the nationalized variety in which the State benefited from the autarkic trends in the period before the War and from socialist tendencies after 1945, launched national companies with the goal of retaining in the country the most important share possible of the reinsurance cessions. This movement ran parallel to the merging of primary insurance companies. It is noticeable that the Anglo-Saxon countries and Switzerland remained outside this tendency. In those countries, reinsurance retained a favourable place in the free market economy.

During the years of crisis, reinsurers had lost a substantial amount of premium income. Numerous factors had contributed to producing this result. First, currency depreciations seriously affected the business of many companies in the gold bloc countries, though the currency realignment had to some extent readjusted the position back towards the old level. Companies also lost quite a substantial amount of fire business, because ceding-offices technically require less reinsurance protection. Moreover, the ceding companies had been keen on increasing their net retentions, on writing inward reinsurance business and in demanding reciprocity at every possible opportunity. Some professional reinsurance companies, controlling direct-writing companies, had been able through those associate companies to indirectly grant reciprocity, but others, not so favourably placed, had had no choice but to offer in retrocession some part of their business. In this case, some reinsurers had had to suffer a double reduction in premium income: first a reduction in gross premiums, and secondly a reduction in net premiums by an artificial increase in their retrocessions over and above technical requirements.

Much business had also been lost during the years of crisis owing to adverse underwriting results making it prudent to reduce commitments, often to the entire exclusion of the branch except for such treaties as might have had to be taken along with good business. This treaty-linking, which was understandable enough from a practical point of view in terms of the treaty with the individual company or reinsurance as a whole, was regrettable, as it made it very difficult for reinsurers to apply curative measures to one branch or another as long as a substantial part of the business could be placed under the cloak of the treaty-linking.

Marine insurance in 1929 was nearing the end of a series of unsatisfactory results, the severity of which had in part been caused by the net premium system preventing the reinsurer from ascertaining the total amount of deduction from the original premium, and thus preventing him from finding out that the net rate ceded to him was hopelessly insufficient. Collapses of important companies at the beginning of the crisis led to a reduction in marine reinsurance commitments by many professional reinsurers, some of them practically retired from the business. Those who remained in the market with reduced commitments had had the satisfaction of observing that an exceptionally favourable claims experience enabled them to make a profit, in some cases even a higher profit than their ceding offices, which meant that commissions paid by reinsurers were now frequently inadequate in the face of their own high costs. It is, however, unlikely that the reinsurers had entirely recovered what they had lost in the years up to 1929, and the falling level of the premium rate represented a general uneasy feeling that claims would rise in the near future. It had certainly not acted as any encouragement to push reinsurers to reconsider their attitudes and re-enter the reinsurance market to any appreciable extent.

In accident, third-party and motor insurance, business had had to be surrendered of unsatisfactory development, and this applied also to other branches such as credit insurance.

The voluntary or involuntary reduction in premiums income was one of the chief features of the period, but there had been other substantial causes of diminished revenue in the numerous conversions of public debt directly reducing the profit on investments. This affected reinsurance companies to no little extent, since they rely upon their investments for the accumulation of contingency reserves to face up to urgencies that could arise in years of catastrophe.

In the main, professional reinsurance companies had followed the development of the insurance industry as a whole. During the years of world crises, they had shown astonishingly good results, enabling the great majority of them to record a stronger position at the end of 1935 than at the beginning of the crisis in 1929–30. Of course, reinsurers have had difficulties with accident and third-party, and occasionally with other branches and with substantial investment currency losses. Yet the improvement in fire reinsurance results since 1929, the black year for European fire reinsurance, has been so remarkable in many countries that the profit on fire reinsurance has been sufficient to cover heavy losses suffered on other occasions. In fact, claims in some countries had fallen so low that there had been inevitable repercussions on premium rates, with the danger of still greater reductions reminding the reinsurers and insurers that a few years of light claims experiment do not necessarily mean a permanently lower claim.

Conclusion

Again, during the whole period under review, the factors that could explain this tendency were both economic and cultural. Nationalism and monetary problems showed how difficult it was for the international reinsurance industry, which was by nature a bridge between the markets to resist the breakdown of international multilateral relations and the trend towards the closeness of the economies themselves or in the frame of the empires.

So far as international reinsurance was concerned, some features of great importance appeared during the inter-war periods. Firstly, and paradoxically, the backlash after the first globalization during the years preceding the First World War had had as a consequence the spread of reinsurance, more or less backed by the respective states. In the new countries that appeared after the War, and in the older countries, there appeared the trend of the rise of intervention of the states. This was notably the case with the setting up of reinsurance monopolies, as for example in South America.

Secondly, new risks appeared or were developed in relation to improvements in industry and, generally, with economic growth. These new risks had as a consequence new fields of activity for insurers and therefore for reinsurers. Such movements lead to a shift in the respective weight of the reinsurance branches. Since fire reinsurance remained the traditional domain of the reinsurers, life reinsurance came to occupy the first rank. Automobile and engine reinsurance rose, as did aviation reinsurance.

Nevertheless, during the period under review professionals held discussions about the health of the reinsurance industry. This may be explained by the relatively slow growth experienced during the period taken as a whole, one of war and crisis, and then by the decrease in ¨aliments¨ to insure and reinsure. It can be also explained by the relationship between direct insurers and reinsurers fighting over the price of premiums. Thirdly, to counter the trend of the time towards weakening the links between traditional partners and also between markets, and as an answer to the organizational changes in insurance, many reinsurers expressed their willingness to build informal or even formal organizational structures linking them.

From Actuaries to Scientific Research

The Evolution of Risk Assessments at the Munich Re

Christopher Kopper

Already before World War I and during the first 30 years after its establishment in 1880, Munich Re became world biggest reinsurance company and gained a global range encompassing Europe and North America. In 1895, the premium income from the Russian insurance market (2.7 million mark) even exceeded the income from the home market in Germany (2.5 million RM)[1]. The management of Munich Re decided to engage in Russia after they had gained a favorable impression of how the Russian primary insurers were managed. But confidence in the managerial abilities of their foreign counterparts was not everything. In the fire insurance branch, Munich Re had to accept different risk structures than in western and central European cities. The centers of many Russian cities except St. Petersburg and Moscow were still dominated by wooden houses that generated high fire risks. As a consequence of frequent town fires, British insurances had retreated from the Russian fire insurance market.

Many files of Munich Re were destroyed after World War II because of storage problems and as a consequence of ignorance and indifference. Therefore, Munich Re's risk assessment strategy of this time is difficult to reconstruct. The first strategy was monitoring the underwriting habits of direct insurers. Munich Re's senior managers traveled to Russia regularly and examined the underwriting principles of their Russian clients. The second strategy was based on knowledge through experience. At this time, the old districts of German cities – and even of big cities like Hamburg, Nuremberg and Frankfurt – still consisted of half-timbered houses with higher probabilities of fire damages. Several big city fires in German and Swiss cities (Hamburg 1842, Glarus 1863) made reinsurers aware of the

---

1 Johannes Bähr and Christopher Kopper (2016), *Munich Re. The Company History 1880-1980*, Munich, C.H. Beck, p. 55.

probability of a huge damage cumulation[2]. The calculation of premiums was based on ex-post knowledge about the frequency of fires (annual damages per 1,000 insured buildings) and the average amount of damages (in percent of the insured value).

Already before 1914, fire insurances could build their premium calculations on long-term damage observations. Statistics of fire insurances distinguished between different hazard classes like buildings with stone or wooden walls and buildings with hard (brick, concrete or slate roofs) or soft covers (timber and thatched roofs). Even some natural hazards like hail with distinct damage variations (relation 4: 1) over the course of a decade were already insurable. Hail insurances compiled sufficient statistical evidence about the average level of damages and maximum respectively minimum annual damages. Based on these statistical compilations, hail insurances built sufficient reserves to stay liquid after a year with a high damage level[3].

German insurance companies started to offer storm damage insurances after the turn of the century. As a consequence of insufficient experiences with the probability of storms and their potential impact on buildings, they consulted storm statistics from meteorological institutes to build their premium calculations on experience. However, meteorological storm statistics of this time did not provide sufficiently accurate information for the calculation of premiums. Insurances had to use experience-based piecemeal engineering (trial and error) to readjust their premium level to the actual damage ratios. Despite the fact that hail and storm damages fluctuated over the course of years, insurers were confident that their statistical evidence over minimum, average and maximum damage levels and the stochastic probability of maximums sufficed to hedge the incalculable probability of these natural hazards.

The only way to prevent deficits between damage coverage and expenses was the regular adjustment of premiums to costs. Reinsurance contacts were usually closed for a year and up to renegotiations if the results for the direct insurer or the reinsurer were insufficient. As the responsibility for the clients' premiums solely rested in the competence of the primary insurer, reinsurances found themselves on the dependent side. But the commission for the direct insurer proved to be an effective lever to adjust the reinsurers' revenues to the damage/premium ratio. A lower commission for the direct insurer left a greater percentage of the overall premium to the reinsurer and prompted direct insurers to increase their premiums.

However, the reinsurers' ability to enforce a more favorable partition of premium income depended on their position in the insurance market,

---

2 Peter Borscheid *et al.* (2014), *Swiss Re und die Welt der Risikomärkte*, Munich, C.H. Beck, p. 228; Eleonora Rohland (2011), *Sharing the Risk. Fire, Climate and Disaster. Swiss Re, 1864-1906*, Lancashire, Carnegie Books.

3 Alfred Manes (1913), *Versicherungswesen*, Leipzig, B.G. Teubner, p. 371-375, 383-386, 414. Alfred Manes was one of the foremost scholars for the insurance sector.

on competition between reinsurers and the necessity for direct insurers to share their risks. Munich Re managed to build a strong position on the world reinsurance market and relied on its ability to negotiate acceptable contracts.

Before the First World War, Munich Re would not have risen to the position of the world reinsurance champion without its success on the US reinsurance market. Munich Re benefited from its position as the first mover among its major competitors. After taking up the American business in 1892, Munich Re soon conquered the position of the market leader. Munich Re was fortunate to appear right in time at the most dynamic economy of the *belle époque.* With a total premium revenue of 25.7 million mark in 1906, the US market emerged as the single biggest market of Munich Re, second only to the home market in Germany (38.5 million). Never before and after did Munich Re generate such a huge percentage (35.2%) of her total premium revenue on a single foreign market[4].

The few surviving files of Munich Re do not reveal the risk perception of the American fire insurance market. Major city fires like the Great Chicago Fire of 1871 only seemed to repeat in a time span of 30 years. Even the Great Baltimore Fire of February 7, 1904 with an insured record damage of 304 million marks did not prompt Munich Re and other European insurers to a partial disengagement from the American market. Munich Re was confronted with net claims of four million marks, about twice its annual profits for 1903/04, but less than 20% of her US premium revenue. But despite the fact that the scale of destruction – about 2,500 buildings – exceeded European city fires of this time by far, insurance managers did not assume that the major factors for the scale of disaster (high winds and a high spatial concentration of value) would spell unbearable risks in other American cities[5].

Insurance managers at this time were particularly unaware that the geological risk of an earthquake spelled destruction for fast growing San Francisco. A prior major earthquake in 1857 had not been recognized as a serious potential threat. Although the Lisbon earthquake of 1755 was still present in the cultural memory of educated Europeans, the temporal distance of 150 years betrayed the still rather unknown fact that earthquakes occurred randomly and unpredictably, not regularly. The potential scale of a major earthquake in California was unknown, since the exact measurement of seismic amplitudes had just recently started. The Richter scale as a standardized measure for earthquakes was not invented before 1935.

4 Bähr and Kopper, *Munich Re*, p. 58-61.

5 *Ibid.*, p. 64-77.

The San Francisco earthquake of April 18, 1906 brought the unprecedented destruction of 28,000 houses. Indirect damages through fire exceeded direct seismic damages by far, as the city was still dominated by highly inflammable wooden buildings. Despite the fact that standard US fire insurance policies did not include cover for earthquake and earthquake-related damages, American fire insurers had to yield to public expectations and the Californian State Superintendent of Insurance who pressed for a complete coverage. Reinsurers like Munich Re could not maintain the contractual exclusion of earthquake-related damages. In regard of the paramount importance of the US reinsurance market and its resolution not to abandon this segment, Munich Re had no choice but to maintain the trust of American insurances and compensate all damages. Thanks to Munich Re's financial strength, the overall claims payments of 11 million marks did not induce an equity loss and did not challenge Munich Re's position as a global leader in reinsurance.

Consequently, the German reinsurers formed an "Earthquake Committee" that worked out a court-proof contractual clause for the future exclusion of earthquake-related damages. This exclusion clause was even integrated into German insurance law in 1908. But on the Californian insurance market, direct insurers and reinsurances had to accept their customers' expectations not to rule out earthquake coverage. Consumers' power proved to be stronger than the proven skepticism of insurance actuaries.

The San Francisco earthquake demonstrated the incalculable ("aleatory") character of geophysical hazards like earthquakes and volcano eruptions and reinforced the fundamental skepticism about the insurability of this kind of natural hazards. San Francisco conformed the skepticism of insurance actuaries that both frequencies and amplitudes of earthquakes were unpredictable. A dependable calculation of earthquake premiums based on probabilities and Probable Maximum Damage (PML) assessments was proven impossible. In 1917, Munich Re was relieved from the cognitive dissonance between the heuristic impossibility to insure earthquakes and the necessity to stay on the Californian insurance market. The United States declared war on Germany, blocked all German assets and withdrew the concessions of German insurances. World War I finished Munich Re's presence on the American, the Russian and the British insurance market and relegated the world biggest reinsurance company to the status of a continental European enterprise. As a consequence, the impossibility to implement a worldwide earthquake exclusion clause had become a problem of the past and fell into obsoleteness.

On its domestic market in Germany, Munich Re was still confronted with occasional claims to include flood losses into the coverage of home insurance. Both MR and direct insurers argued that floods were unpredictable in frequency and size – and therefore uninsurable. Even heavy flood events like the North Sea flood of February 1962 did not prompt the government to press for a comprehensive coverage and to mandate the inclusion of flood risks. Munich Re was not confronted with the challenge to calculate flood risks before providing home reinsurance in countries where flood coverage was included.

World War I and Germany's post war hyperinflation limited the regional scope of Munich Re to Germany, the former Central Powers and the neutral nations of Europe. After 1923, Munich Re re-gained a foothold in the Western European reinsurance business. Due to the sequestration of her American assets, the Munich Re did not succeed in re-establishing a foothold on the American market during the 1920s and 1930s. But the territorial reduction from a global to a European player did not prevent Munch Re from re-attaining the position of world's biggest reinsurance company until 1936.

World War II re-limited the spatial field of the Munich Re to the countries under German occupation and the neutral nations of Europe. Thanks to an elaborate camouflage scheme, Munich Re managed to continue business with some pro-allied countries in and outside Europe even during the war. The Zurich-based Union Rück, a 100% affiliate company of Munich Re, acted as a trustee and stepped into several hundreds of Munich Re's foreign reinsurance contracts.

After Germany's unconditional surrender, the United States and Great Britain prevented German reinsurances from re-entering foreign markets until 1950. But the re-globalization of Munich Re already started off in the early 1950s. Unlike the 1920s, the Munich Re managed to enter markets in South East Asia and Japan. The re-emergence of the Munich Re as a global player can be explained by the fact that her professional reputation as a knowledgeable and dependable insurance had not been affected by the National Socialist foreign trade and foreign exchange policies. Second, the Munich Re emerged as an innovative reinsurer with a greater determination to take new risks than her biggest competitor Swiss Re. During the 1950s, the Munich Re became the first mover in the world wide re-insurance of industrial machinery[6].

Since the beginnings of reinsurance in the 19th century, re-insurance was a knowledge-based and highly internationalized business. But until the 1950s, the management of the Munich Re was dominated by lawyers, and not by engineers, mathematicians and scientists. So far, the application of higher math was limited to a field of insurance where mathematical skills had been applied since the 19th century: Life Insurance. Until the

[6] Munich Re Corporate Archive (HAMR), Rote Sammlung, No. 606, 19 December 1962.

1960s, the only mathematicians at Munich Re worked in the life department. Their task was to examine the premium calculations of direct life insurances for accuracy and dependability. The knowledge of life insurance mathematicians expanded with progress in stochastics, but did not significantly change until the 1960s. Munich Re's non-life departments borrowed their mathematical expertise from the life department before they hired their own mathematicians in the early 1970s.

In the mid 1960s, the introduction of the first IBM computers provided life insurances with the opportunity to recalculate and update mortality statistics. Newly calculated premium scales took account of the increase of life expectancy and allowed for premium reductions. Life insurances in countries with obsolete mortality statistics received updated statistics from Munich Re as a quid pro quo for retrocessions[7]. The statistical knowledge and the computer capacities of the Munich Re became important tools for the acquisition of new clients in the life insurance business. In many lesser-developed nations, dependable mortality statistics were either obsolete or entirely missing. Life insurers in lesser-developed countries often charged higher premiums than necessary. Since 1965, Munich Re offered life insurers to calculate updated national mortality tables. This kind of computer based statistical counseling proved to be an important tool to gain new life insurances as clients[8].

In the non-life fields of insurance such as home and liability insurance, the statistical knowledge for premium and reserve calculations was applied by actuaries without university degrees in math. Actuaries were insurance professionals with statistical skills, but without research qualifications. Their knowledge of damage probabilities was generated through the statistical analysis of damage events. This kind of knowledge was stochastic and based on ex-post experience. In the German-speaking world of the 1930s to 1950s, research literature on applied math in non-life insurance was limited to a rather thin reference publication[9]. This reference book did not introduce readers into the world of advanced probability calculations and mainly referred to Gauss and Pearson curves.

If damage probabilities were underrated, future losses could be prevented through annual re-negotiations and re-adjustments of premiums and commissions. Re-insurance contracts were closed on an annual base and were routinely canceled by the reinsurances for re-negotiations. Reinsurers avoided operating deficits through the ex-post adjustment of the

7 HAMR, Rote Sammlung, No. 744 (22 September 1965) and 802 (2 November 1966).

8 HAMR, Rote Sammlung, No. 802, 2 November 1966, No. 982, 27 May 1970.

9 Paul Riebesell, *Einführung in die Sachversicherungsmathematik* (Berlin: Mittler & Sohn, 1936); see also Max Gürtler, *Betriebswirtschaftliche Probleme des Versicherungswesens* (Wiesbaden: Dr. Th. Gabler, 1959), 131.

premium level to the damage level. Since the beginning of the 1970s, Munich Re perfected the adjustment of direct insurers' commissions to the damage/premium ratio with a flexible commission scale. This meant that the direct insurer's commission depended on the development of the damage/premium ratio. Commissions increased when the damage ratio improved and decreased after the damage ratio deteriorated. When the damage/premium ration of Munich Re exceeded 73.5% (after provisions to the direct insurer), Munich Re employed a readjustment clause in order to reduce the direct insurers' commission[10]. This regulation ensured a quick adaption of commissions to the damage level and facilitated a fair burden sharing between direct insurers and reinsurers.

Globalization confronted the Munich Re with challenges to its traditional underwriting principles. Re-insurance companies like Munich Re and Swiss Re had developed a long-standing practice of the exclusion of "bad" risks. Until the 1960s, Munich Re and German direct insurers consequently excluded incalculable geological risks like earthquakes and unpredictable weather-related risks like flooding from coverage. But during the beginnings of globalization in the 1950s and 1960s, Munich Re experienced a perforation of the borderline between the "good" and the "bad" risks. Munich Re had to adapt its non-admittance policy of "bad" climatic and geophysical risks to the demand structures of non-European insurance markets and to the expectations of foreign clients. Even in some European insurance markets, the Munich Re had to accept the regulatory standard to include comprehensive weather-related risks – like flooding – into standard home insurance contracts.

The US affiliate of Munich Re followed a cautious underwriting policy ("profits before volume"), but could not decline to re-insure the hurricane insurance contracts of the American direct insurers. In a similar case, Munich Re had to admit earthquake risks on the growing reinsurance market in Japan. Globalization pushed the limits of re-insurance and forced the Munich Re and its competitors to deal with risks they had previously perceived as incalculable. The activities of the Munich Re outside Europe triggered significant learning effects. Through their presence on the Japanese market, Munich Re managers learned a lot about risk cumulation control in earthquake areas[11].

The unknown risk structures of non-European markets were important push factors to build sophisticated databases for the regional prob-

---

10 Letter of MR to Victoria Insurance, 22 October 1971, in: HAMR, Schwarze Sammlung, new draft of guideline E7 on the PML.

11 Martin Herzog (1974-1992), *Was Dokumente erzählen können – Zur Geschichte der Münchener Rück*, Munich: unpublished typoscript, p. 1137. In Munich Re Corporate Archive.

abilities of climate-dependent weather hazards and geological risks. The experience-driven actuary knowledge of non-life insurances was falling behind the epistemological challenges of the global (re)insurance business. As a consequence, the Munich Re started to establish scientific research units for the assessment of geophysical and climatic risks during the 1960. The infamous hurricane "Betsy" (September 1965) made havoc in a formerly unknown scale of 1.4 billion US$ in several southern states (Alabama, Louisiana, Mississippi). 59 years after the San Francisco earthquake, this was the first non-European catastrophe that left a dent in Munich Re's balance sheet. At this time, Munich Re was already exposed to hurricane damages in the US by its position as the ninth-largest American reinsurer. Munich Re had to cover gross damages of 6.4 million DM ($1.6 m)[12]. But it should take until the early 1970s until the non-life branches of Munich Re started to employ sophisticated stochastic knowledge for the calculation of damage probabilities. The success of global reinsurance required more than solid knowledge of national and international insurance law and the actuary monitoring of premium/damage coefficients. Since the scale of losses from natural catastrophes grew exponentially, reinsurances faced the challenge to upgrade their prognostic capacities. In 2005, Hurricane "Katrina" caused damages of $108 billion, about a hundred times the size of "Betsy". The steep increase of damages was less the effect of inflation than a consequence of increased concentrations of values in industrial buildings, private homes and in material infrastructures of all kind.

During the 1960s, Munich Re and its most important competitor Swiss Re worked on making property insurance more scientific. Experts from property insurance departments of both insurers discussed their experiences with the use of mathematical models in premium calculations. The annual Monte Carlo meeting of reinsurance executives in 1968 highlighted the anxieties about the limits of traditional insurance knowledge[13]. Reinsurance executives admonished their peers to a more intensive exchange of information.

But at this time, Munich Re and Swiss Re had already begun a shift from the retroactive and purely stochastic determination of risks to future-oriented causal research of risks. Munich Re rated earthquake risks according to observed earthquake losses. Newly hired geophysicists analyzed all available contemporary descriptions of earthquake damages since 1900 and calculated their magnitude according to the Richter scale. This method allowed Munich Re to set up a long-term database of earthquakes, reaching even back to the time when precise seismographic measurements

12 HAMR, minutes of the supervisory board meeting on 10 November 1966, in AR-P/43; see also Rote Sammlung, No. 776, 4 May 1966.

13 Borscheid *et al.* (2014), *Swiss Re*, p. 215-220.

did not yet exist. The specific expert knowledge of geophysicists made it possible to convert observed magnitudes into an exact scale and to extend the series of measured magnitudes far into the past.

This scientific competence was highly important for catastrophic events that repeated very irregularly and during long time spans. This knowledge allowed MR to develop calculations of earthquake probabilities on a wider base of observations that significantly raised the stochastic precision of forecasts[14]. By calculating earthquake risks, Munich Re also developed prognoses about the future probability of severe earthquakes. The geophysicists at Munich Re expected one or even several severe earthquakes in Japan to happen between 1975 and 1985. Consequently, the management began checking the accumulated risk on the Japanese market in order to limit its net risk. Munich Re employed a hedging strategy, generously retroceded XL branches and umbrella covers at Lloyds and reduced the gross risk from 100-160 million to only 15 million DM[15]. But the next decades revealed that neither statistical extrapolations nor geophysical prognostics could provide dependable results with a high probability of occurrence. To the surprise of statisticians and geophysicists, the first major earthquake struck Japan in 1995 – in Kobe. Thus, earthquakes remained highly incalculable risks.

Data sets on the danger of earthquakes allowed better risk calculations and helped to align premiums. In order to generate higher premium revenues, Munich Re was ready to share scientific evidence with primary insurers. When Munich Re's data sets yielded a lower probability of serious earthquakes, direct insurers gained agency to lower premiums to the benefit of their competitiveness and their policyholders. Sharing knowledge generated a win-win situation for both direct insurers and reinsurers and became an important tool to market reinsurance services.

The global activities of Munich Re triggered the need for meteorological expertise. The necessity for meteorological knowledge became particularly evident on the Australian market. After a series of natural catastrophes like heavy floods, tornadoes and bush fires, the Insurance Council of Australia started to compile a cumulative zone plan for the frequency of extreme losses due to weather related catastrophes. Munich Re became involved because of its presence on the Australian market since the 1960s. As a consequence of severe weathers, Munich Re had to bear high actuarial losses in property insurance. For this reason, Munich Re was eager to support research efforts of Australian direct insurers. Munich Re was one of the few insurances worldwide with an in-house meteorolo-

14 Discussion between MR and Swiss Re on 12 June 1979, in. Swiss Re Corporate Archive, No. 10.135.225.02.

15 Minutes of the board meeting on 21 April 1975, in: HAMR, V-P/27.

gist. The management sent the meteorologist to Australia in support of the Australian insurance industry[16]. The behavior of Munich Re was not purely altruistic. The management hoped to improve the dependability its own weather prognoses through a collaborate research effort and was definitely interested in helping Australian insurers to improve their pricing and underwriting policies. Lower losses of direct insurers promised better results for the reinsurers.

The employment of a meteorologist was the first step towards a corporate climate research department. Until the 1970s, meteorological catastrophes like hurricanes and floods were still perceived as non-periodical damage events that were neither man-made nor followed a long-term trend. After scientists discovered hard evidence for a coincidence between increased carbon-dioxide levels in the atmosphere and a global warming, Munich Re extended its research department and appointed climate experts to the staff. As a global reinsurer, Munich Re was immediately confronted with the consequences of global warming phenomena like El Niño, which increased the danger of tropical storms and hurricanes.

The emergence of new technologies formed another push factor for the integration of scientific and technological knowledge in the reinsurance industry. When the first jet planes were introduced into civilian aviation around 1960, primary insurances and reinsurance companies were confronted with the challenge to assess the risk structure of an unknown technology. As a consequence, primary insurances assessed this new and unpredictable risk very cautiously and started with high insurance premiums[17].

The problem of the unknown risk behavior of jet planes was even aggravated by missing experiences with cumulative risk structures. A plane crash does not only involve comprehensive coverage for the plane loss. Plane crashes induce cumulative risks like life insurance claims for passengers and crew members and third party liability for damages of other planes and of ground installations at the crash site. The loss of cargo and luggage was the last, but not always the least problem if valuables and hazardous materials were involved. Following the traditional piecemeal engineering process of the insurance industry, insurances determined the premium level on the base of previous accident rates – which turned out to be considerably lower than expected. Due to their unexpectedly favorable claims experience after the commercial introduction of jet planes, direct

[16] HAMR, Rote Sammlung, No. 1315, 17 November 1976.

[17] HAMR, Rote Sammlung, No. 408, 13 May 1960; No. 480; 24 February 1961; No. 549, 17 November 1961.

insurers dropped the comprehensive insurance premium by 0.5% each year at the beginning of the 1960s[18].

Munich Re's major competitor Swiss Re got the impression that Munich Re managed to offer more aggressive quotes thanks to its highly knowledgeable staff in the aviation department. A lack of empirical experience was compensated by well-funded knowledge of a new technology and its risk behavior in order to offer lower, competitive rates. Munich Re applied a similar approach of educated risk estimates at the beginning of the 1970s when the aviation industry introduced the Boeing 747 ("jumbo jet"). In this case, the insurance industry was not confronted with a genuinely new technology but with the challenge to assess a significant higher PML.

The demand for scientific knowledge became most evident for the insurance of nuclear power stations. As a consequence of their high value and their unprecedented – and unknown – risk potential, primary insurances and reinsurances had to form national insurance pools to ensure a sufficient coverage. High, even euphoric expectations about the future of nuclear energy fueled insurers' anticipations of a high demand for coverage. In 1957, five years before the first German nuclear reactor became operational, it already became apparent that the German insurance industry was reaching the limits of knowledge about what was insurable. The Probable Maximum Loss (PML) of reactor equipments and buildings in case of the largest assumable nuclear accident could still be calculated by the methods of machine insurance. Due to the lack of experience with this new technology, insurers could not calculate the frequency and the average length of operational interruptions in case of accidents. The limits of knowledge were even more challenged in regard of liabilities for third party damages. The insurance pools for nuclear power stations had no experience with the probability, the scale and the impact of the possibly largest nuclear fallout. At first, the liability risk for a nuclear fallout did not seem to be insurable, because there were no experiences with the financial consequences of personal damages and the effects of long-term radiation in the vicinity of reactors. Insurances like Munich Re shared the common optimism about the feasibility of nuclear energy and the trust in nuclear engineering, but had to transcend their traditional, experience-driven methods of risk assessment.

Munich Re recognized that assessing the risk of nuclear reactors went beyond the expertise of its mechanical engineers. The board member in charge of machine insurance could not help but confessing that insur-

---

18 HAMR, Rote Sammlung, No. 655, 4 December 1963.

ances had to assess unprecedented risks[19]. Munich Re could only close the knowledge gap between their lack of experience and the challenges of a totally new technology by hiring professionals with highly specialized expertise. In 1968, Munich Re hired a nuclear physicist with a Ph.D. degree to provide professional expertise for the risk assessment of nuclear power stations. At this time, statistical experiences in the operation of commercial reactors were still limited, since they were still based on a few first generation prototypes. The serial production of reactors hat not yet begun in Germany, Europe and the United States.

Nuclear power stations were the first technological artefacts which confronted reinsurances with the financial limits of private liability insurance. At first, the German nuclear insurance pool limited liability coverage to an amount of only 10 million DM per reactor. In 1963, the supranational European nuclear agency EURATOM obliged the member countries to ensure a minimum liability coverage of 20 million DM by the national insurance pools[20]. In order to provide sufficient coverage for the possibly largest fallout, the German federal government stepped in for the insurance industry and covered all liabilities beyond 20 million DM up to a maximum of 300 million DM per reactor. The insurance of nuclear power stations would have failed if the national governments had not provided a liability ceiling up to the highest damage assumption of this time. Already in 1966, the liability ceiling of the commercial insurance pool proved to be too low for the first generation of commercial reactors. Shortly after the second German commercial reactor in Obrigheim began operations in 1968, the methodological problems in the assessment of the Probable Maximum Loss became evident. Munich Re doubted the estimate of Germanys biggest direct insurer Allianz that the PML would not exceed 40% of the insurance sum for the entire reactor plant. The employment of a nuclear physicist paid off: Thanks to his expertise, Munich Re came up with a new and less optimistic estimate[21].

But at that time, Munich Re and direct insurers still shared the optimistic assumption of the nuclear industry that a reactor might never be totally destroyed or totally unusable due to radiation damages. The 1979 nuclear accident at the Harrisburg power plant "Three-Mile Island" should prove them wrong and prompted a readjustment of prior PML calculations. Before the Fukushima catastrophe of 2011, Harrisburg was the first major nuclear accident in the western world to demonstrate that

[19] Klaus Gerathewohl (board member of MR): Neue Schwerpunkte für die technischen Versicherungszweige. Attachment to the minutes of the 313th supervisory board meeting on July 10, 1969, in: HAMR, AR-P/44.

[20] Christoph Julian Wehner, Grenzen der Versicherbarkeit – Grenzen der Risikogesellschaft, *Archiv für Sozialgeschichte* 52 (2012), 581-605.

[21] Minutes of the technical executive meeting on 11 November 1968, in HAMR, V-P/4.

a total destruction of a reactor – at least in insurance terms – could happen. Since the reconstruction of the Harrisburg reactor was estimated at $440 million, the whole insurance sum of $300 million did not suffice for a full damage reimbursement. For the first time ever, Munich Re incurred a loss of 5 million DM in the relatively small but usually profitable nuclear property insurance[22]. But unlike Fukushima, the Harrisburg accident did not involve third party liability.

Despite the fact that the unexpected case of a total destruction had happened, Munich Re's CEO Horst Jannott utilized the unexpected reactor accident as an opportunity to demonstrate the fundamental trust of German insurers in the safety and insurability of nuclear power plants[23]. At this time, the liability of the German nuclear insurance pool was limited to a maximum of 500 Million Deutschmarks per reactor. The ostentatious demonstration of trust did not distract the German government from drawing a different conclusion. The government sought to increase the operator liability from 500 million DM to two or even to three billion DM. At this point, the German nuclear insurance pool reached the capacity limit for the first time. Munich Re demonstrated its readiness to increase coverage in order to demonstrate unshaken confidence in nuclear energy, but regarded 1.5 billion DM as a capacity limit[24].

Despite their public demonstration of trust, German insurance managers harbored uncertainty whether to offer unlimited liability coverage like the American insurance industry. The accessible files of Munich Re do not reveal if their in-house nuclear experts did not – or could not categorically rule out a major catastrophe which might explain their reticence to offer unlimited cover. Only in 1985, one year before the Chernobyl accident, did the German government raise the operators' liability to 2.5 billion DM per reactor. All third party damage beyond this limit was still externalized and to be covered by the German government.

The integration of scientific knowledge into the calculations of reinsurers had two major causes. The first cause was the natural tendency of reinsurances to enlarge their markets through globalization and the ensuing confrontation with a great variety of unknown risks. The second cause was technological innovation and the challenge to assess new technologies with unknown risk behaviors and potentials. As the traditional managerial and legal knowledge of the insurance industry was reaching its limits, insurance executives had no choice to consult professionals with a wide

22 HAMR, Rote Sammlung, No. 1443, 12 April 1979; No. 1463, 29 August 1979; No. 1495, 18 April 1980; No. 1527, 28 November 1980.

23 Horst Jannott, Einige aktuelle Kernfragen der Assekuranz aus der Sicht eines Rückversicherers, *Versicherungswirtschaft* 34 (1979), 283-286.

24 Wehner, *Grenzen der Versicherbarkeit*, 601.

range of scientific expertise. The decision to establish permanent in-house research units instead of commissioning external research institutes can be explained by the motive not to share this knowledge with competitors. But reinsurances like Munich Re were willing to share their newly generated knowledge in order to create the joint benefit of dependable premium calculations and to establish long-term cooperations.

Conclusion

The risk assessment procedures of Munich Re followed a distinct learning curve. Right after the establishment of Munich Re in 1880, the company hedged the contemporary peril of huge losses through city fires with a globalization strategy. Munich Re established the global distribution of risks as a tool to avoid an over-exposure to local risk accumulations. The global risk distribution strategy helped Munich Re to level out the unparalleled losses through the San Francisco earthquake of 1906. But the major learning effect of the San Francisco earthquake was the conclusion to exclude geophysical risks from coverage. Munich Re established a permanent firewall between calculable – and therefore insurable – risks like fires and incalculable and uninsurable risks like floods, volcano eruptions and earthquakes.

As a consequence of two world wars, Munich Re was banned from the non-european insurance markets until its international reestablishment in the 1950s. At the end of this decade, Munich Re was confronted with two different challenges to the traditional, non-scientific risk assessment procedures. The first challenge was the transition to the nuclear and the jet age, the advent of two new technologies with unknown risk behavior. The second challenge was Munich Re's appearance on the American and the Asian reinsurance markets and the confrontation with new forms of natural hazards. Munich Re needed new technological in-house expertise to assess the Probable Maximum Losses and the accident probabilities without prior empirical knowledge. During the 1960s, Munich Re began to base its underwriting expertise on sophisticated knowledge in civil engineering, mechanical engineering and even aviation and nuclear technology, added by scientific expertise in geophysics and meteorology.

Swedish Life Reinsurance and Risk Management

Mats Larsson & Mikael Lönnborg

Introduction

The purpose of the reinsurance industry is to provide insurance for primary insurers. The latter party cover life and non-life risks among corporations and individuals through different technical calculations. In the field of life insurance, insurers makes estimations based on mortalities tables, the current and possible future interest rates and operation costs, and sometimes on medical judgements of individual persons, to set the premium. In some cases people are considered to be a higher risk than average and are refused to sign an insurance contract, but other insurers might to an increased premium also cover these so-called substandard risks.

Primary insurers have fairly standardised policies, whereas those of reinsurers are often less so, more internationally oriented and likely to cover very large risks. There is little doubt that primary insurance policies, as well as an insurance market based on fixed premiums, would be difficult to sustain over the long run without reinsurance. Reinsurance enables portfolio diversification by the primary insurer in order to avoid the kinds of devastating losses that could threaten its survival[1].

The issue of reinsurance does of course have a strong link to direct insurance. The reinsurance business proceeded from the primary activities of the various insurance companies, as well as their need to minimize the associated risks. In the Nordic countries the first joint-stock companies in the field of

---

1 Edwin Kopf, "The Origin and Development of Reinsurance", (Proceedings of the Casualty Actuarial Society, 1929); Cecil E. Golding. *A history of reinsurance with sidelights on insurance* (London: Sterling, 1930); Neil Doherty and Kent Smetters, "Moral hazard in reinsurance markets", *Journal of Risk and Insurance*, 72/3 (2005), 375-391; Harold James *et al.* (eds.), *The Value of Risk. Swiss Re and the History of Reinsurance* (Oxford: Oxford University Press, 2014). Peter Borsheid and & Niels. V. Haueter (2012), *World Insurance. The Evolution of a Global Risk Network*, Oxford, Oxford University Press; Klaus Garethewohl (1980 and 1982), *Reinsurance. Principles and Practice*. Vol. 1 & 2, Karlsruhe, Versicherungswirtschaft.

insurance emerged in the 1850s and initially they covered their reinsurance needs through bilateral agreements with mostly foreign insurers, in particular from United Kingdom, Germany, France and the Netherlands. For instance, Skandia, the first Swedish joint-stock insurer founded in 1855, set its risk limit at SEK 100,000 (US$ 1 million in 2016 prices) for either a fire or life policy. Any insured amount above the limit was redistributed to other companies[2]. Thus, reinsurance allowed a company to accept extensive risks without jeopardizing its survival.

The development of reinsurance in the Nordic countries were divided into two different trajectories during the late 19th century, on one hand concerning the non-life reinsurance and on the other hand the life reinsurance. In the first case, the larger insurers founded daughter companies that exclusively dealt with non-life reinsurance but also continued with bilateral agreements. In the latter case, a couple of life reinsurance companies associated with direct insurers were established but none of these corporations survived for very long, and bilateral agreements became the solution for direct life insurers until the early 20th century[3].

This chapter will discuss the emergency of the first solution concerning life reinsurance in the Nordic countries – which later on became copied in the entire Nordic area – namely the Swedish life reinsurance market and how it emerged from the mid-19th century ant developed until the 2010s. As noted, in the wake of the founding of the first joint stock corporations in the middle of the 1850s, insurers set rather limited risk maximums and signed reciprocal treaties with mainly foreign insurers to limit their risks. However, this mainly concerned non-life insurance portfolios, while the issue of life reinsurance was far more complicate to cope with. During the following six decades life reinsurance was handled by individual corporations but in 1914 a common owned by domestic life insurers, reinsurance company – Sweden Re was organised to deal with the issue for reinsurance for the entire market. This meant a monopoly situation for life reinsurance in Sweden and no other company was doing business in this area, that continued until the end of the 1980s when most of the individual insurers preferred to set up their own corporations for dealing with reinsurance.

This chapter will give a broad and long-term analysis of the Swedish life reinsurance market with special emphasis on the organised risk management through the jointly owned corporation Sweden Re, why it emerged, how it developed and how and why the co-operation was dissolved. We will concentrate on important changes on the market but the entire story

---

2 Mikael Lönnborg (1999), Internationalisering av Svenska försäkringsbolag. Drivkrafter, organisering och utveckling, Uppsala, Uppsala Studies in Economic History.

3 Karl Englund (1940), *Återförsäkringsaktiebolaget Sverige 1914-1939. Redogörelse för bolagets verksamhet under de tjugofem första åren*, Stockholm, Ivar Haeggströms.

of the company Sweden Re and the Swedish life reinsurance market is available in Larsson & Lönnborg (2014). In this chapter, we will address events of special importance, thereby reflecting the development of the entire Swedish life reinsurance market since 1914.

Background

The first joint stock insurance company in Sweden, Skandia in Stockholm, was founded in 1855. The company was a mix selling both non-life and life insurance and two additional mixed companies were also founded Svea in Gothenburg 1866 and Skåne in Malmö 1884. The first pure life joint stock insurance company was Nordstjernan, established in 1871, followed by Thule in 1872 and Victoria in 1882. In the end of the 1880s a large number of mutual insurance companies began to emerge, in particular with the purpose to widen the customer base. In 1899 mutual industrial life companies was founded that sold "small insurances" among the working class. This type of insurance products grew very quickly and already in 1901 the joint stock insurers founded a company, De Förenade (the united) to compete with the mutual insurers. De Förenade and in particular the CEO, Filip Lundberg, would later play a significant role in the construction of the life reinsurance company Sweden Re. In addition, most of the mentioned corporations would in the end join the co-operation within the life insurance market and as owners of Sweden Re[4].

By the end of the 19th century, the life insurance market had expanded considerably, followed by growing competition between joint-stock and mutual companies. However, in the legislation of 1903 the two different insurance forms, became supervised equally and this opened up for a completely new kind of co-operation on the market. The most important organisation in this field emerged in 1906 under the name of the *Svenska Livförsäkringsbolag Direktörsförening* (Association of Swedish Life Insurance Executive Managers, the word managers was dropped in the 1930s). This organisation was of great importance not only for setting rates but also for putting together rules of conduct and stabilising the expanding insurance market[5]. This association was crucial in realising the construction of the life re-insurance company Sweden Re.

---

4 Mats Larsson and Mikael Lönnborg (2014a), *SCOR Sweden Re. 100 Years of Swedish (Re)Insurance History*, Stockholm, Dialogos.

5 Filip Lundberg and Harry Molén (1958), *Utvecklingslinjer inom svensk livförsäkring*, Stockholm, Svenska Livförsäkringsbolags Förening; Mats Larsson, and Mikael Lönnborg (2016), "Regulation competition of Swedish Insurance Business. The Role of the insurance cartel registry", in Susanna Fellman and Martin Shanahan (eds.), *Regulating*

The establishment of Sweden Re

Sweden Re was a matter of fact created as a means of cleaning up the life reinsurance market in Sweden and was to some extent an entrepreneurial venture, maybe not from a traditional point of view but nonetheless it was something new that emerged in collaboration. At the end of the 19th century and the beginning of the 20th century, several life insurance companies were founded; however a large number of them were underfinanced and had problems surviving. One measure to finance the business was through accepting reinsurance treaties from foreign insurers (in particular from Germany, however which companies it concerned its not mentioned in the sources) that on the positive side generated a lot of income at an early stage. But the construction could be very costly in the long run and the companies could suffer severe losses. In the case of bankruptcies among small life insurance companies, the confidence for the entire market could be jeopardised. In addition, it was regarded as important to limit the outflow of capital from Sweden through foreign reinsurance, and instead supply capital for the domestic industry[6].

Several life reinsurance companies were started from the 1890s and onwards with close connections to a single company but none of these survived, mainly because they were too dependent on only one company and it was difficult to expand the business. In addition with the previous mentioned dilemma of small companies expanding through unfavourable treaties with foreign insurers, this started a discussion about founding a domestic life reinsurance company as a joint venture among Swedish insurers. Mainly two individuals discussed this issue, namely Filip Lundberg – the CEO of the industrial life insurer De Förenade, jointly owned by major insurance companies – and Paul Bergholm – CEO of the minor life insurance company Brage that suffered partly from previously written reinsurance contracts. In particular Filip Lundberg urged for a reinsurance corporation jointly owned by the directly operating life corporations in order to simplify the procedures of reinsurance and reduce disadvantages of competition. The idea was that the reinsurance should be arranged on a risk-premium basis and that the company should retrocede as much as possible of its risks to the shareholding companies. After intensive negotiations with the managing directors of

Competition: Cartel Registers in the Twentieth Century World, Abingdon & New York, Routledge, p. 248-267.

6 Paul Bergholm (1925), ***Återförsäkringsaktiebolaget Sverige 1914 11/11 1924***, Stockholm, Återförsäkringsaktiebolaget Sverige; Karl Englund (1945), "*Märkesmän inom svenskt försäkringsväsen. Biografiska snabbteckningar*", Stockholm, Gjallarhornet; Karl Englund (1993), *Skandiamän och andra försäkringsmän 1855-1970. Femtio biografiska studier*, Stockholm, Skandia.

the leading life insurance companies at the time, it was possible to launch the idea of a life reinsurance company jointly owned by Swedish life insurance companies. The 13 shareholders were required to contribute share capital in relationship to their reinsurance operations, see table 1.

Table 1: Shareholders of Sweden Re with year of establishment, 27 October 1914

Insurance company	Capital paid up (SEK)	% of share capital
Thule (1872) JS	120,000	20
Nordstjernan (1871) JS	85,000	14.2
Skandia (1855) JS	80,000	13.3
Svea (1866) JS	70,000	11.7
Svenska Lif (1891) M	51,000	8.5
Victoria (1882) JS	35,000	5.8
Allmänna Lif (1887) M	35,000	5.8
Skåne (1884) JS	30,000	5.0
Balder (1887) M	28,000	4.7
Oden (1889) M	23,000	3.8
Nordpolen (1897) JS	18,000	3.0
Svecia (1898) M	15,000	2.5
Allmänna Pension (1898) M	10,000	1.9
TOTAL	600,000	100

Note: JS=joint stock, M=mutual. Source: Bergholm (1925).

Sweden Re became not only an instrument for sorting out the issue of reinsurance but an organisation that contributed to and facilitated collusion on the market. The fact that Sweden Re's CEO Paul Bergholm also became a member of the boards of the Swedish Association of Life Insurers and the Swedish Insurance Society (later on chairman) as well as editor-in-chief of the magazine Scandinavian Insurance Quarterly also indicated that Sweden Re was part of the organised co-operation among Swedish insurers. The other initiator, Filip Lundberg, did only participate at the board of directors during the early years of Sweden Re. The reason was that he was CEO of the industrial life insurance company De Förenade that only wrote so-called small insurances and did not practise any reinsurance. Lundberg had written a dissertation about the issue of reinsurance and his ideas of redistributing collective risks were the foundation of Sweden Re.

However, he returned to the board meetings of Sweden Re in the 1930s when he became CEO of the life insurer Victoria[7].

The establishment of Sweden Re made the reinsurance market more effective compared to previous founded small company owned reinsurers. It reduced both the risks and the costs connected to life reinsurance, and as it turned out also increased the possibilities for the life insurer to broaden their market into new customer segments. At the time, the actors within the insurance market tried to solve common problems through collusive actions in concord, and Sweden Re was an excellent example of that.

Setting up the business and development until 1949

The establishment of Sweden Re was thus an initiative by members of the Association of Swedish Life Insurers. The large companies were well represented on the board, and several of Sweden Re's initiators had privileged long-term positions. Bergholm stayed on as CEO and board member until 1950, while Edvard Phragmén (Allmänna Liv) was chairman from 1914 to 1937.

An important issue faced by the new company was to draw up principles for premium rates. Two different rates had been calculated in early December 1914 based on actuarial tables used by 17 life insurers. Reinsurance agreements were proposed to reflect those principles. The risk premium alternative was accepted by all insurers and approved on 17 December by Sweden Re's board, making it the guiding principle for all traditional reinsurance in the country[8].

Initially, Sweden Re only accepted risk premium reinsurance, built on the theories of the co-founder Filip Lundberg but already in 1915 the business expanded through another collaboration measure. At the time over 80 per cent of private life insurance applications were accepted without any problems, however, the remaining 20 per cent represented a problem. One of the deputy board members suggested that Sweden Re should set up an Appraisal Council to evaluate applications that had been rejected. If Sweden Re assumed the responsibility of evaluating all the applications that had been turned down by its affiliates, a joint strategy could be established making it possible to avoid needless competition, not to mention the advantages for prospective policyholders.

Another three life insurance company joined the arrangement and thus, 16 life insurers adopted the principles of substandard risk in 1915.

7 Grenholm and Cramér, *Utvecklingslinjer i svensk livförsäkring.*

8 Bergholm, *Återförsäkringsaktiebolaget Sverige.*

The event was also a kind of combat against unfair competition. For the system to be sustainable it was important that all substandard risks be reported to Sweden Re and that the insurers avoided competing with less satisfactory risks or withhold information about potential risks. This was not always the case, and Sweden Re had to remind the affiliated companies of their pledge on several occasions. There were cases when certain companies accepted substandard risks, instead of transferring to the pool administrated by Sweden Re, as a way of expanding the portfolio. Adoption of reinsurance with substandard risks was an important step towards a life insurance system that would be accessible to the general public. It also opened the eyes of insurance managers to the need for proactive analysis of various medical risks. Several life insurers committed themselves to the promotion of medical research for the purpose of revising premium rates. The result was impressive almost 90 per cent of all substandard risks was accepted, meaning that life insurance became available for people with medical problems (in particular associated with tuberculosis and heart diseases), without increasing the level of risks among Swedish life insurers[9].

For making the business sustainable, international contacts were of course important for Sweden Re in order to guarantee proper risk distribution, and international insurers continued to collaborate during World War I. Relationships with other Scandinavian insurance companies were vital to Sweden Re in terms of both reinsurance and information sharing. The personal contacts that the company's founders and board members had established abroad were invaluable. Among the first retrocession arrangements were with Atlas, Münchener Rück, Kölnische Rück, Wiener Rück and the Gjenforsikring. The German, Norwegian and Danish companies were particularly important. Sweden Re also concluded retrocession agreements in 1917 with Norske Folk (later Storebrand) in Kristiania (Oslo) and Dana in Copenhagen, setting the stage for Scandinavian collaboration. These companies had used Sweden Re as a blueprint when structuring their organizations. A retrocession agreement was also signed in 1919 with Varma (later Retro), a new Finnish reinsurer.

The selection of partners became more important during the financial crisis of the early 1920s. Several international insurers suffered economic setbacks, but Sweden Re escaped unscathed because it had signed its retrocession agreements with relatively stable companies. In addition, Sweden Re cancelled – just before the hyperinflation in Germany 1923 – several arrangements with German insurers and concluded new treaties

9 Mats Larsson and Mikael Lönnborg (2014), *SCOR Sweden Re*, Stockholm, Dialogos Förlag.

with British reinsurers, and had wisely turned down an offer to participate in a retrocession arrangement with American insurers (because it turned out to be a portfolio with extensive losses). In the 1920s the CEO Paul Bergholm travelled around Europe for signing new treaties and opened up bank accounts in Paris, Brussels, Amsterdam, Zürich, Prague and Madrid[10].

The assumption of substandard risks also broadened Sweden Re's international network. Norway and Denmark were major markets, providing contacts that were later instrumental in setting up similar companies abroad. There were also discussions of forming a mutual substandard insurer covering all of Scandinavia. But the national approach turned out to be better, given the near monopolies that the reinsurers enjoyed in their domestic markets. Based on the business of Sweden Re, similar companies were also established in Germany (Die Hilfe) and Austria (Verband zur Versicherung anormaler Leben).

Thus, the business of Sweden Re showed a steady growth but again the aim was neither to seek highest possible growth nor profit, instead to make sure that the owners, the life insurance companies, could diversify their portfolios. However, after fifteenth years of operations, the share capital had been repaid to owners through dividends. Again, we have to stress that the logic for Sweden Re was not to seek the highest possible expansion and the company only grew in accordance with the need of the direct insurers. Indeed, the company was part of the system to facilitate collusion on the Swedish market, and should not be regarded as a normal corporation seeking highest possible return. This would change in the beginning of the 1990s when the business was transformed, however, this practice of business is one explanation why Sweden Re did not developed in the same way as for instance Swiss Re and Munich Re. There are several other explanations as well, but we will return to them in the conclusion.

In 1937 three additional companies, Valand, Folket (later Folksam, the co-op insurer) and Framtiden, became new shareholders. As seen in Figure 1, risk premium reinsurance dominated the portfolio until the 1940s, but in 1944 the premiums in substandard reinsurance skyrocketed through a couple of new treaties. Since 1930s Sweden Re had accepted minor treaties that were not risk premiums or substandard – defined as 'other insurance'. During World War II Sweden Re also administrated a war risk pools, including Swedish volunteers in the so-called Finnish winter war 1939-40. In addition, Sweden Re administrated reinsurance of life policies from every company in Denmark and Norway during the German occupation 1940-45.

10 Englund, *Återförsäkringsaktiebolaget Sverige.*

Figure 1: Annual premiums from risk premium reinsurance, substandard reinsurance and other insurance, 1915-1949, million Swedish crown, current prices

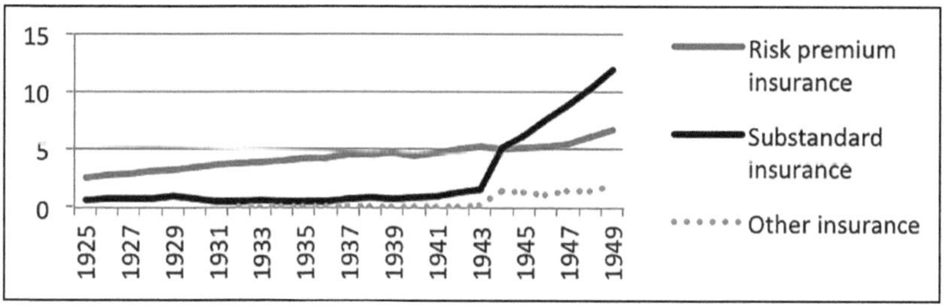

Source: Sweden Re, annual reports, 1915-1949.

The consolidation between 1950 and 1980

The Swedish insurance market consolidated between 1950 and the mid-1980s. This changed the ownership structure of Sweden Re, but also transformed market conditions. The Swedish economy during the period from 1950 to 1979 was among other things characterized by the regulation of financial markets. The measures were initiated and managed by the Swedish Central Bank (Riksbank). While banks and insurance companies were being placed under the same rules, institutional changes both limited and expanded opportunities for new activities. The growth of the social security system impacted the structure of insurance services. Thus the market for traditional life and pension insurance did not expand very rapidly, while group pension and special occupational plans were increasingly important. Both reinsurers and direct insurers were affected[11].

The 1950s was a difficult period – Sweden Re's business did not expand very rapid, and the problems accumulated in the late 1950s. The insurance market, particularly occupational pensions, was going through a period of uncertainty, and as long as no political resolution had been achieved, the prospects for both private life and pension insurance remained murky. However, several changes during the 1960s and 1970s set the stage for the life reinsurance market and made it possible for Sweden Re to recover. Expansion to new areas was one major change. An agreement to manage the assets of Swedish Medical Association – disability insurance – was a big boom for the company. The other major change was the extension of its

[11] Mats Larsson and Mikael Lönnborg (2010), "The History of Insurance Companies in Sweden: 1855-2005", in Leonardo Caruana de las Cagigas (ed.), *Encuentro Internacional sobre la Historia del Seguro*, Madrid, Fundació Mapfre, p. 197-237.

already existing activities. The growing risk premium policies, which had dominated Sweden Re's reinsurance business in the 1910s, decreased in importance from the 1940s to the late 1970s as substandard risk coverage grew in stature. The policyholders' premiums for substandard risk reinsurance fell sharply in 1960 after the mortality rate among these groups had been low for several years. Although the reductions applied only to new reinsurance agreements, previous policies received a correspondingly higher bonus. Fluctuations in mortality rates affected both reinsurance of substandard risks and risk premium insurance[12].

From the late 1960s the group of other insurances also started to increase fast. At the late 1970s premium incomes from other insurances exceeded those of the risk premium insurance and especially important were the reinsurance of disability insurances. Along with the dominance of substandard reinsurance, the trend reflected the growing importance of private insurance in the welfare system and the ability of Sweden Re to adjust to the changing face of the market. Alongside its reinsurance business, Sweden Re sold small direct group life and ordinary insurance.

Figure 2: Annual premiums from risk premium, substandard and other insurance, 1950-1979 (million SEK)

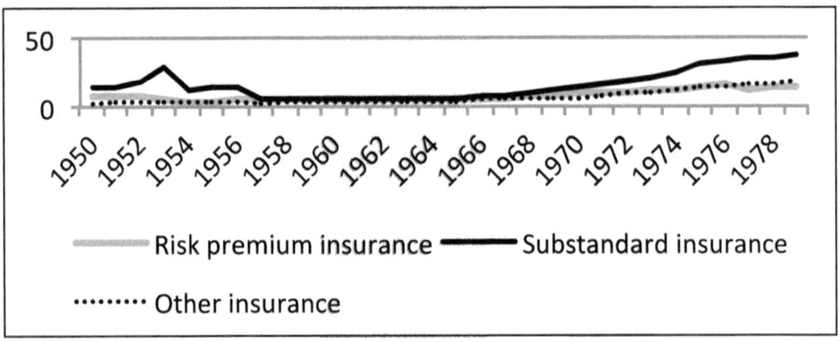

Source: Sweden Re, annual reports 1950-1979.

Concentration of the insurance market

Consolidation of the insurance market began shortly after World War II, when insurance companies increased their co-operation within groups, but at the same time working under their own name. This co-

12 Larsson and Lönnborg, *SCOR Sweden Re*.

operation also opened the door to survival and development of cartelisation of Swedish insurance. However, when companies in the 1960s started to merge, the number of life insurers declined, as did the number of owners of Sweden Re.

During the following decades, three mergers of special importance for Sweden Re were completed. The first one in 1965 created the Skandia Group, which was a merger between all large joint-stock insurance companies (Englund, 1982). The second merger in 1971 between a number of large mutual companies created the Trygg-Hansa Group, and the third merger in 1985 resulted in the Wasa Group, and consisting of mutual companies. These three companies were, together with Folksam, the owners of Sweden Re in the late 1980s, with Skandia dominating the ownership with around half of the shares of Sweden Re. But with four large owners, the preconditions for keeping the ownership of Sweden Re together deteriorated[13].

The global challenge

Sweden Re had been created to solve life reinsurance for the majority of the Swedish life insurers. Together with substandard reinsurance, the reinsurance of ordinary life and disability insurance had built up the business of Sweden Re, and the market was still more or less the same in the 1980s. But with the deregulation of international financial and insurance markets, the possibilities to change the business and the challenges from the global market increased. Since Sweden Re's clients had developed from Swedish companies to international business groups, the possibilities to find other reinsurance solutions had increased.

In order to survive this global challenge, Sweden Re had to be more adapted to international standards and traditions. Otherwise the risk for a liquidation of Sweden Re would be an immediate alternative – as had happened with fellow subsidiaries, dealing with life reinsurance in the Nordic countries. The consolidation of the reinsurance market to fewer companies was an international phenomenon that was based on deregulation of inter-

---

13 Mats Larsson and Mikael Lönnborg (2007), "Ömsesidig försäkringsverksamhet och den svenska försäkringsmodellen", *Scandinavian Insurance Quarterly*/1, p. 85-100; Mats Larsson, and Mikael Lönnborg (2009a), "Den svenska finansmarknaden i ett långsiktigt perspektiv", in Gunvall Grip (ed.), *Folksam 1908-2008. Mer än endast försäkring, volym 2*, Stockholm, Informationsförlaget, p. 210-255. Mats Larsson and Mats Lönnborg, "Samverkan och konkurrens inom svensk försäkring", in Gunvall Grip (ed.) (2009b), *Folksam 1908-2008. Mer än endast försäkring, volym 2*, Stockholm, Informationsförlaget, p. 179-209.

national markets and the flow of global capital between countries. These larger reinsurance companies with extensive capital assets could undertake larger business agreements and reduce risks for their clients.

After the deregulation of the Swedish financial and insurance markets, institutional preconditions also favoured an international development for Sweden Re. However, the problems were – as already mentioned – the lack of capital and international inexperience. Connected with this was also the strong tradition of the regulated Swedish insurance market with remnants of the strong Swedish regulatory tradition. Taking this into consideration, it might be surprising that Sweden Re managed to survive and develop.

In the 1980s only four owners in Sweden Re remained – due to the extensive wave of mergers in the industry – Skandia (50 per cent), Trygg-Hansa (32 per cent), Wasa (15 per cent) and Folksam (3 per cent). All four owners had extensive foreign business and had started to accept life reinsurance abroad, and the co-operation through Sweden Re was making less and less sense. The discussions about the direction of Sweden Re were closely linked to the activities of the owners, particularly Skandia. Thus, an application to the Insurance Inspectorate for authorization to reinsure substandard risks from Skandia International became a turning point. Initial communication with the board suggested that the application would be approved and that Skandia would gradually transfer its reinsurance agreements from Sweden Re to the subsidiary. Sweden Re's management was concerned that the other owners might take similar steps, or follow the recent trend of retaining more risks in-house. In addition, the Swedish Competition Authority regarded the joint ownership of Sweden Re as an outdated construction that would not be acceptable when joining the European Union – which was finalized in 1995[14].

The future of Sweden Re was threatened at the end of the 1980s, when the shareholders (in particular Skandia and Trygg-Hansa) preferred to deal with life reinsurance within their own organizations. For finding new business, Sweden Re for instance started to serve as a consultant to new insurances companies but the owners were particularly averse to the idea. The management of Sweden Re was looking for solutions, and even discussed the possibility of buying out Skandia or otherwise becoming more independent. But such a step would make it harder to retain a position on the reinsurance market. Restructuring Sweden Re as a mutual insurance company might be a way of reducing owner influence and that also was discussed. Another solution would be to restructure Sweden Re

---

14 Mats Larsson and Mikael Lönnborg (2016), "Regulation competition of Swedish Insurance Business. The Role of the insurance cartel registry", in Susanna Fellman, and Martin Shanahan (eds.), *Regulating Competition: Cartel Registers in the Twentieth Century World*, Abingdon & New York, Routledge, p. 248-267.

as a holding company such that each activity would be a separate business. Given the turbulent market in 1987-1988, management was on the outlook for new activities. Four of the alternatives discussed at their June 1988 meeting were particularly interesting:

- obtaining a concession to provide direct life insurance
- expansion in the European reinsurance market
- taking over claim settlement for certain types of policies that had low priority among direct insurers
- introducing some kind of credit reinsurance for unit-linked policies.

However, the problem was resolved in November 1989 when Skandia, Folksam and Trygg-Hansa announced that they wished to end their partnership with Sweden Re and either divest their holdings or liquidate the company. Following a series of negotiations, Wasa offered to buy out the other three owners and make Sweden Re a subsidiary of Wasa International, the group's non-life reinsurer. An agreement was signed in January 1990 and as of 1 July, Wasa was the sole owner of Sweden Re. Skandia and Trygg-Hansa phased out their remaining business, while Folksam continued to reinsure some of its substandard risks with Sweden Re.

Criticism in the media and by the Consumer Ombudsman of Sweden Re's role in cartelization of the Swedish life insurance market (evaluating substandard risks on behalf of other companies) contributed to the ownership changes. With Wasa as the sole owner and the other large insurers performing their own risk analyses, such criticism lost its cogency.

International owners and market development

The Swedish insurance market has experienced revolutionary changes over the last 25 years. Several large Swedish joint-stock insurers have been transformed and ownership changed. For instance, Trygg-Hansa merged with the Swedish bank SEB in 1997; the life insurance operations were kept but the non-life portfolio was sold to Danish Codan – in turn owned by British RSA. In addition, Skandia separated and later sold its non-life portfolio. Furthermore, the remainder of Skandia was taken over by Old Mutual in South Africa, but the Swedish part of the group was later purchased by the subsidiary Skandia Life and transformed into a mutual insurance company in 2014. In addition, due to the financial crisis of the 1990s, the lack of capital and losses on international insurance, all Swedish insurance companies withdraw from international business and instead focused on the domestic market[15].

The ownership and business changes sharply reduced substandard reinsurance activities. Approximately two-thirds of premium income from such reinsurance dried up. Life surplus reinsurance declined more than one-third, while other types of reinsurance remained unaffected. In figure 3 the development of Sweden Re illustrates that the business grew the entire 1980s but when Wasa became the sole owner, the portfolio diminished considerable. Total premium income and retrocession premiums dropped considerably in both 1990 and 1991. Sweden Re faced a completely new situation. Globalisation and competition were now the name of the game. If the company was to survive, new business areas would have to be established in line with the trend among reinsurers abroad.

In the 1990s, Wasa International – the sole owner of Sweden Re since 1989 – suffered major losses, and in order to make the company competitive in the international market, it was necessary to have a major infusion of capital. Considering the financial crisis at the time, it was difficult to obtain resources from the capital market, and in the end, the decision was to withdraw from the international market and put the business in run-off. This in turn made the ownership of Sweden Re questionable and Wasa started to look for a buyer of all or parts of the company.

The first option was Eureko Re, but after a due diligence process demonstrating that Sweden Re was too dependent on business generated from Wasa, this transaction failed. The second and realised transaction in 1995 was with the German Gerling Group, and the problem of being too closely connected to Wasa was solved through a co-operation agreement, where Wasa promised to remain a minority owner for a five-year period. In short, the new ownership structure of Sweden Re was a blessing in disguise for the company. Sweden Re was transformed into a competitive reinsurance company with higher shares of reinsurance premium kept for own account, and the entire business was restructured. Being part of an international financial group – and changing its name – also meant access to international capital.

15 Mats Larsson and Mikael Lönnborg (2010), "The History of Insurance Companies in Sweden: 1855-2005", in Leonardo Caruana de las Cagigas (ed.), *Encuentro Internacional sobre la Historia del Seguro*, Madrid, Fundació Mapfre, p. 197-237.

Figure 3: Sweden Re, total wreinsurance amount received, broken down by types of reinsurance (SEK million) 1980-1994

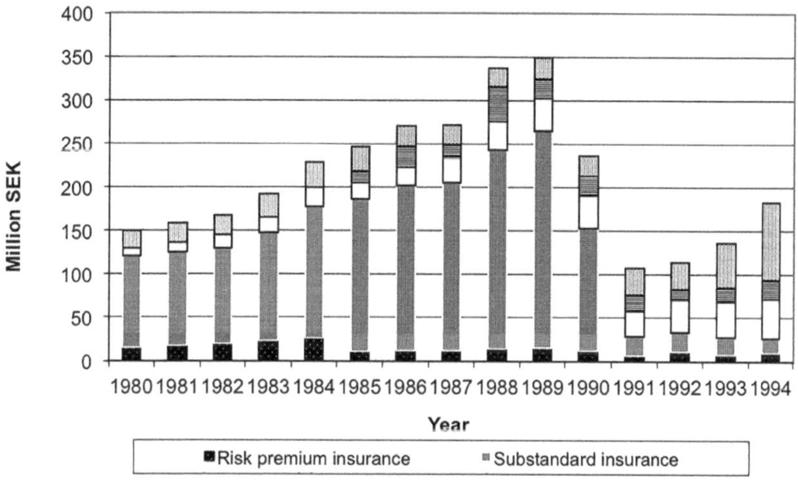

Source: Sweden Re, annual reports 1980-1994.

The change of Sweden Re can be illustrated by the fact that for the first time ever in the company's history a marketing department was constructed within the company. Sweden Re started to focus not only on negotiations but also on selling, that entailed a lot of changes of the logic of the business. The reinsurance portfolio in the mid-1990s for Sweden Re could be divided into one Swedish 'non-profit' reinsurance program and one international commercial program. In addition, one 'service program' existed that had been set up as a captive reinsurance system where Sweden Re acted as an administrator. The strategic plan for 1995–96 entailed a lot of different goals and projects; the most important goals were to cancel the non-profit program, build up a marketing unit and facilitate reporting systems in order to decrease administrative work. In addition, the company expanded also to the Scandinavian countries, in particular in Norway[16].

The financial difficulties for the parent company Gerling were result of the recession after 9/11 2001 but also due to heavy losses in motor liability insurance and asbestos claims in the United States, and the losses continued. These problems made it necessary in September 2002 for Gerling to stop writing any new non-life reinsurance, but life reinsurance operations continued. In spite of the financial turmoil at the Gerling Group and the transformation into the company Revios, Sweden Re showed an

16 Mats Larsson and Lönnborg (2014b), *Finanskriser i Sverige*, Lund, Studentlitteratur.

outstanding performance. The uncertainty about the future of Revios and the group was finally solved through a takeover by the French company SCOR in 2006. Again, Sweden Re became part of an international financial group, and today the SCOR Group is the fifth largest reinsurance company in the world.

Sweden Re has managed to adapt to changing ownership structures which has resulted in a reorganisation to cope with a wider compliance scheme, improved routines and increased reporting demands, which is a natural consequence of being part of an international group noted on several stock exchanges. The last major change is that Sweden Re, instead of being a subsidiary, became a branch of SCOR in 2013.

When foreigner owners entered Sweden Re the business was transformed completely. The company experienced a fairly stable market until the mid-1990s, but with changes in ownership, the possibility to generate profit from the companies' business enhanced. The growing business volume was of course closely connected to the boom in the international market and possibilities to develop the Sweden Re's business.

To sum up, it has been crucial for Sweden Re to be part of a viable international financial group to make the company a competitive player in the life reinsurance market. This would have been possible with a Swedish owner with a large international portfolio, but considering that every Swedish insurance company had withdrawn from international business, this was in practice impossible. We can therefore state that without foreign owners – Gerling, Revios and finally SCOR – Sweden Re would most likely have been eliminated from the market before the celebration of the first 100 years of business.

A major change has thus since the 1990s occurred on the Swedish life reinsurance market. Today, the market is not a monopoly market – which of course is impossible since Sweden entered the European Union in 1995 – and most of the larger life insurers deal with their own reinsurance. Beside Sweden Re, the larger reinsurers on the market are Hannover Re and Swiss Re, demonstrating that the life reinsurance market has transformed considerable the last 25 years, and that Swedish life reinsurance today faces international competition.

Figure 5: Sweden Re, premium gross and retrocession in SEK million 1995-2013

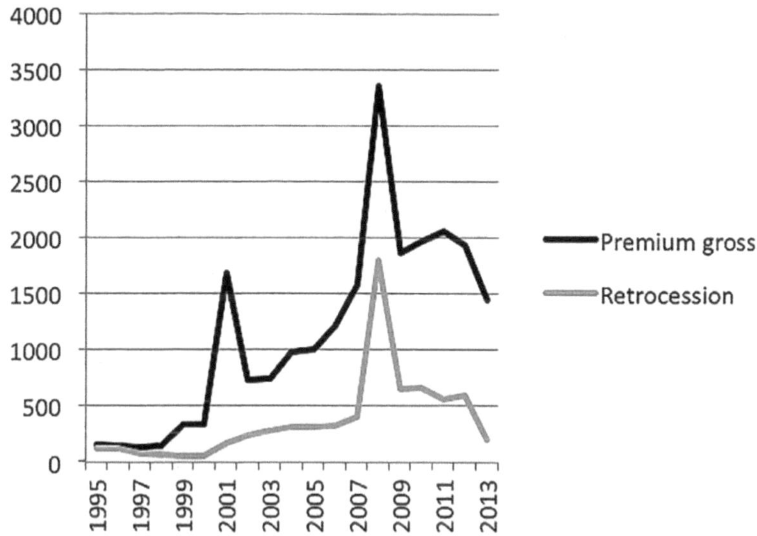

Source: annual reports, 1995-2013.

Concluding remarks

The Scandinavian countries have during the last century constructed many odd features on the financial market, and indeed the way of solving the issue about life reinsurance through a monopoly company owned by almost the entire market, was one of them. Sweden Re was created to solve the immediate problems of the Swedish insurance market, but the long-term effects were considerable and influenced the reinsurance situation in Sweden for over 70 years. During these years, Sweden Re had a more or less monopoly position in the Swedish life reinsurance market. This gave stability, which is of the greatest importance for trust among both insurers and reinsurers. But this also distanced Sweden Re from developing new areas – which was not requested by the owners –. And with voluntary and legal restrictions on profits and dividends, Sweden Re became more of a service organisation than a market-oriented company.

Although Sweden Re was not the first reinsurance company to do business in Sweden, none of its predecessors survived for very long. Sweden Re was founded as a joint venture by a number of Swedish life insurers to handle their reinsurance requirements and limit their risks. The reinsurance business proceeded from the primary activities of the various insurance companies, as well as their need to minimize the associated risks. Insurance companies set a risk maximum, and any insured amount above the limit was redistributed to other companies. Thus, reinsurance allowed a company to accept extensive risks without jeopardising its survival[17].

In the anniversary book of Sweden Re in 1965 (p. 7), Tage Larsson summed up what had characterised Sweden Re during the first fifty years of business:

> In fact, to a great extent the problems of [Sweden Re] have been less complicated than those of the most other companies, since the company is more concerned with mortality than with the value of money and interest rates, more with ideas than with mass work, and more with negotiating than with selling.

He continued by arguing that there were four main reasons that could explain why Sweden Re had become the central institution for life reinsurance in Sweden and an efficient 'servant' of life insurers. First of all, the high propensity to co-operate – in spite of fierce competition – among the Swedish life insurers; otherwise a construction like Sweden Re would not be a possible solution for the market. Second, the high scientific standard of mathematicians, medical experts and risk assessors connected to Sweden Re. Third, the successful selection of CEOs of Sweden Re, which has been crucial in gaining legitimacy in the market. Fourth, the prominent technical methods developed by Sweden Re, in particular the idea of reinsurance on a risk premium basis that initially was a true innovation.

Of course, the context of Sweden Re's business has changed over time. No longer is the company solely a servant of Swedish life insurers, and nowadays the marketing aspects have become of more importance for the business. The ownership structure is of course totally changed, and that has made aspects of co-operation in the Swedish market obsolete. The market has been widened outside Sweden, mainly to Norway but also with minor engagements in Denmark and Finland. Still, the appointment of CEOs has been successful and managing directors have shown remarkable longevity, and developing innovative technical methods has continued to be at the heart of Sweden Re's success formula, in the meaning of successfully distributing the risk portfolio to its owners, primary insurers.

The solution of the creating a common owned – both by joint stocks and mutual insurers – corporation to deal with the issue of life reinsurance through monopoly was a Scandinavian solution. Sweden Re was founded in 1914 and similar organisation – using Sweden Re as a blueprint – was a couple of years later created in Norway (Norske Folk) and Denmark

---

17 Sven Palme (1923), *Thule under 50 år*, Stockholm, Hæggström; Bergholm, *Återförsäkringsaktiebolaget Sverige*; Englund, *Återförsäkringsaktiebolaget Sverige*.

(Dana). The sister organisation has disappeared through mergers with larger domestic insurers and regarding that Sweden Re now is branch office of multinational corporations, the company have today a complete different business than in the 1980s.

Especially when the two largest groups, Skandia and Trygg-Hansa, started to develop their own solutions for reinsurance, and the need of, and interest in, keeping Sweden Re as a partner evaporated. The arrangement was finally broken when these companies decided to develop their own reinsurance companies and either sell their shares or close down Sweden Re. Folksam also left the partnership, but kept solving parts of the reinsurance need through Sweden Re, which made Wasa the remaining owner of Sweden Re. When Wasa offered to buy the other companies' shares the survival of Sweden Re was solved for the moment – as a subsidiary of Wasa International.

Thus, consolidation of the insurance market created the foundation for a new ownership construction of Sweden Re, and for the possibilities of developing the business of the company. However, the lack of capital and international contacts, as well as the fact that Sweden Re's owner Wasa was a potential rival to all potential clients, hampered the development and Sweden Re stagnated during the new ownership, and it was not until the company was taken over by foreign owners that Sweden Re's business started to develop faster. In turn, the changes in the end of the 1980s meant that the business of Sweden Re no longer covers the entire Swedish life reinsurance market.

Sweden Re had monopoly rights for the entire Swedish life reinsurance market between 1914 and 1989, when it became a subsidiary to the Swedish insurer Wasa International. Due to heavy losses on the international market and withdrawal from international business, Wasa sold Sweden Re to German Gerling, but kept 49% of the shares during a five-year period. However, due to heavy losses on the American market, Gerling was restructured under name of Revios, and later on merged with SCOR from France. Since 2013, Sweden Re, is a branch office of SCOR, and thereby part of an international group dealing with life reinsurance from the entire world.

The development of Sweden Re demonstrated a very specific path-dependency. During the monopoly period the company acted strictly as a service unit to its shareholders and even though certain new areas of business were included, the shareholders had control over these changes. During the era when Wasa was the sole owner, the premium income hampered for Sweden Re because the cancellations of business from Skandia and Trygg-Hansa. The Gerling era started with a restructuring phase and slowly and then more quickly recovering the premium income but Sweden

Re was again hampered by the difficulties experienced by Gerling. When Scor became the owner, the premium income increased quickly but later on experienced flatten rate of premiums. The path-dependency is that Sweden Re never truly been an independent company, and that is the main reason why the company have not been able to develop in the same manner as for instance Swiss Re and Munich Re.

The Creation of Complex Reinsurance Networks in Spain (1880-1940)

Pablo Gutiérrez González & Jerònia Pons Pons

Despite its relative backwardness, the Spanish insurance industry made wide use of innovative devices developed in mature markets from the beginning of the First Globalisation. Management structures such as the agency system, actuarial elements such as mortality tables and financial instruments such as reinsurance served to change and modernise Spanish insurance during the following decades[1]. Specifically, reinsurance served as an especially useful device since insurance demand was growing in an environment of opening up to international markets, low regulatory requirements and a chronic lack of capital resources[2]. In fact, the 1869 legislation on joint-stock companies and the political stability from 1875

1 The cases studied in Peter Borscheid and Niels Viggo Haueter (2012), *World Insurance. The Evolution of a Global Risk Network*, Oxford, Oxford University Press, constitute a complete analysis of the spreading of such techniques from pioneering countries to the periphery. For the specific case of Spain, see Esperanza Frax and María Jesús Matilla (1996), "Los seguros en España: 1830-1934", *Revista de Historia Económica* 14/1, p. 183-203, for a long-term approach to the performance of the industry. Jerònia Pons (2002), *Las estrategias de crecimiento de las compañías de seguros en España, 1900-1940*, Madrid, FUNEP; and Jerònia Pons (2008), "Multinational enterprises and institutional regulation in the life insurance market in Spain 1880-1935", *Business History Review*, 82 p. 87-114, explain the organisation of life and non-life markets. José Luis García Ruiz and Leonardo Caruana de la Cagigas (2009), "La internacionalización del seguro español en el siglo XX", *Revista de Historia Industrial*, 41/3, p. 17-48, analyse the process of internationalisation of Spanish insurers. Jerònia Pons and Pablo Gutiérrez (2016), "The actuarial practices of British life insurance companies in peripheral countries: the case of Spain (1890-1936)", *Enterprise and Society*, 17/2 p. 237-264, explain the evolution of actuarial techniques in Spain and the implications for multinational companies.

2 Gabriel Tortella *et al.* (2014), *Historia del seguro en España*, Madrid, Fundación MAPFRE. For an in-depth view of legal requirements and capital shortages and an analysis of the results, see Pons, *Las estrategias de crecimiento de las compañías de seguros en España, 1900-1940*, and Jerònia Pons (2007), "The influence of foreign companies in the organization of the Spanish insurance market: diversification and cartelisation 1880-1939", in Borscheid and Pearson (eds.), *Internationalisation and globalisation of the insurance industry in the 19th and 20th centuries*, Zurich, Marburg University, p. 49-65.

converged with a lack of fiscal and financial regulations to create an environment that facilitated the development of insurance. As a result, during the following decades the Spanish insurance industry became increasingly complex, with different actors such as mutual societies and foreign and domestic companies, all utilising quite different reinsurance strategies[3].

Reinsurance allowed companies to deal with increasing underwriting risks in the main branches by making more homogeneous risk portfolios and by reducing loss volatility[4]. Financial literature states that reinsurance helps companies to improve their market position by enhancing their underwriting capacity in spite of capital shortages[5]. Thus, in the case of Spain, domestic companies became competitive despite their low levels of capitalisation; foreign branches operating with minimum reserves could maximise the returns of their head office's investment in Spain; and mutual societies overcame their lack of equity capital by using reinsurance[6]. Nevertheless, this wide use of reinsurance by different actors did not result in a Spanish core of specialist reinsurers. It was only during the extraordinary conditions created by the First World War that a group of Spanish reinsurers was constituted, but it was short-lived.

This chapter aims to analyse the integration of reinsurance in the Spanish insurance industry and to identify the different risk exchange

---

3 Robin Pearson (2010), "Las compañías de seguros en España antes de 1914", in Jerònia Pons Pons and María Ángeles Pons Brías (eds.), *Investigaciones históricas sobre el seguro español*, Madrid, Fundación MAPFRE, p. 101-30, analyses the entry and performance of British companies in Spain. For a description of the reinsurance strategies of British companies, see Robin Pearson (1995), "The development of reinsurance markets in Europe during the nineteenth century", *Journal of European Economic History*, 24, p. 557-72.

4 Klaus Gerathewohl (1993), *Reaseguro. Teoría y Práctica*, Madrid, Reaseguros Gil y Carvajal and Pearson (1995), "The development of reinsurance markets in Europe during the nineteenth century".

5 Financial studies identify reinsurance as an imperfect substitute for capital, since it allows companies to deal with increasing risks without enlarging equity funding or reserves. See David Mayers and Clifford Smith (1982), "On the corporate demand for insurance", *Journal of Business*, 55, p. 281-96, David Mayers and Clifford Smith (1990), "On the corporate demand for insurance: evidence from the reinsurance market", *Journal of Business*, 63, p. 19-40, Lawrence Powell and David Somner (2007), "Internal versus external capital markets in the insurance industry: The role of insurance", *Journal of Financial Services Research*, 31, p. 173-88 and Griselda Deelstra and Eugene Plantin (2014), *Risk theory and reinsurance*, London, Springer.

6 Eugenio Prieto (1973), *El reaseguro: función económica*, Madrid, ICE; Gerathewohl, *Reaseguro. Teoría y Práctica*, Mike Adams *et al.* (2011), "Mutuality as a control for information asymmetry: a historical analysis of the claims experience of mutual and stock fire insurance companies in Sweden 1889-1939", *Business History*, 53, p. 1074-91, and Josef Liljegren and Lars-Fredrik Andersson (2014), "Variation in organizational form across lines of property insurance: Sweden, 1913-1939", *Financial History Review*, 21, p. 77-101, analyse the impact of organisational form on the firm's performance.

strategies implemented by foreign offices, domestic stock companies and mutual societies. To achieve this goal, we use corporate sources from head offices insuring in Spain in order to analyse reinsurance practices, the determinants of the reinsurance decision and its impact on company performance according to organisational, financial, and management features. The remainder of the chapter is organised as follows: section 1 deals with the performance of Spanish insurance in the tumultuous period of the First World War and the development of a transient core of Spanish pure reinsurers. Section 2 analyses the determinants of foreign companies' reinsurance strategies in the Spanish market. Section 3 is focused on the uses of reinsurance by domestic companies and the links with internationalisation and growth strategies. Section 4 draws some conclusions.

The performance of Spanish insurance in the tumultuous period of the First World War and the development of a transient core of Spanish pure reinsurers

During the decades of consolidation of reinsurance as an international business, the Spanish insurance industry experienced a sustained trend of growth and modernisation. Overall economic performance boosted the demand for insurance in different branches, while the entry of foreign capital contributed to standardising the use of new techniques and devices[7]. Moreover, the close links with the international market and the environment of freedom for foreign companies facilitated early contacts between Spanish insurers and some of the world's leading reinsurers and made reinsurance a commonly used device.

Nevertheless, the first pulses of economic nationalism reached the insurance industry in the first decade of the 20th century. In 1908 the first comprehensive regulation for insurance companies was passed, establishing an official registry of insurers to control underwriting practices and financial strategies. Indeed, the new legislation empowered a regulatory agency, the *Comisaría General de Seguros*, to examine and approve the terms and conditions of policies. At the same time, it set minimum capital requirements and the amount of reserves according to the business underwritten. Furthermore, the regulation obliged companies to deposit these reserves in Spanish securities, limiting the possibilities of investment

7 There are no data on premiums for the decades prior to 1900, but from 1870 to 1908 the number of companies rose from 23 to 124, according to Frax and Matilla (1996), "Los seguros en España: 1830-1934".

abroad. This posed several difficulties for the operation of foreign companies in Spain, since one of the pull factors for multinational insurers had been the almost totally free disposal of their assets[8].

These changes were already being implemented when the First World War broke out. As in other neutral countries, the Spanish economy was significantly affected by the changes in the international scenario. In fact, the condition of neutrality put Spanish companies among the main providers of freight and insurance services[9]. Moreover, the rise of premium rates, due to the increase of danger in maritime routes, converged with the rise of the value of insured goods and ships: from 1915 to 1919, premiums underwritten in marine insurance tripled in real terms[10]. Along with these elements, the demand in other lines such as fire insurance grew due to the overall economic performance. As a result, liabilities faced by Spanish insurers increased hugely, while reserves and capital resources remained stable in aggregate terms[11].

Within this context of financial constraints, insurance companies reinsured these new risks abroad as the only way to preserve business balances. The massive purchases of reinsurance in the international market generated increasing outflows of capital that attracted the attention of the regulatory authorities. Indeed, the abrupt changes in the insurance market and the economic nationalism pervading the government led to viewing this process as a drain on the national wealth. Consequently, the institutional framework supervising insurance business was modified by the inclusion of a special Committee on War Insurance.

After a short period analysing the current trends in marine insurance, the Committee was appointed as a permanent body in charge of assuming risks by means of reinsurance with the support of the state treasury. Furthermore, within the new legal framework, the state became the obligatory reinsurer of all war risks underwritten in Spain[12]. In this scenario, marine insurers in Spain searching for reinsurance services

8 Jerònia Pons Pons (2010), "A History of insurance companies in Spain until 1936", in Leonardo Caruana de las Cagigas (ed.), *Encuentro internacional sobre la Historia del seguro*, Madrid, Fundación MAPFRE, p. 141-74, analyses the impact of the new regulations at both financial and managerial levels and the different responses adopted by companies.

9 For a comprehensive description of the effects of the Great War on the Spanish economy, see Carles Sudriá (1990), "Los beneficios de España durante la Gran Guerra. Una aproximación a la balanza de pagos española, 1914-1920", *Revista de Historia Económica*, 8, p. 363-96, and Elena San Román (1994), "Las consecuencias pacíficas de la Gran Guerra: la movilización industrial", *Hispania*, 54, p. 611-58.

10 Jerònia Pons (2002), *Las estrategias de crecimiento de las compañías de seguros en España, 1900-1940*, Madrid, FUNEP.

11 Memoria de la Dirección General de Seguros, Bolsa e Inversiones, Years 1910; 1915; 1920; 1925; 1930; 1935 and 1942-1951 (1954).

12 Law of 2 March 1917, *Gaceta de Madrid*, 3/03/1917, No. 62.

should cede their risks to this Committee which, in turn, would assess the chances to reinsure abroad with equal compensation. At the same time, this system allowed the Committee to access real market information and to exert tight control on prices and conditions included in the policies. In this sense, the high rates of inflation experienced in Spain from 1916 were attributed, among other things, to the performance of financial services such as insurance.

During 1917 and 1918 the scope of action of the Committee was broadened to include ordinary risks in marine insurance. This constituted a *de facto* state monopoly in marine reinsurance, similar to initiatives undertaken in other European countries[13]. The next step, in 1919, was to expand the monopoly to all other insurance branches. In this last case, the imminent end of the war and the doubts arising around the Committee's performance made this resolution short-lived. In fact, criticism of the Committee's work had been increasing since 1916. Liberal politicians, economists and public figures related to the financial industry questioned the Committee's performance and efficiency in dealing with the rise of insurance prices or the outflows of capital[14]. Certainly, the role of the state as a sort of *universal reinsurer* had not been accomplished: the Committee's rate of risk retention dropped from 75% in 1917 to 17% in 1919. These imbalances between risks covered and retroceded transformed the state into a mere intermediary, pushing up prices of services and limiting the normal functioning of the market[15].

However, although state intervention perturbed the performance of foreign reinsurance channels, it was far from dislodging private initiative. The concentration of reinsurance flows through the Committee was parallel to the foundation of five reinsurance companies between 1918 and 1920. These companies were Garantía, Madrid, Esfera, Astur and Centro Español de Reaseguros (Table 1). They applied for authorisation to operate in marine reinsurance and, immediately after the broadening of competencies of the Committee in 1919, in the fire branch.

13 France, Belgium, Sweden, Baltic countries, Argentina and Brazil undertook similar initiatives. James *et al.* (2013), *The value of risk. Swiss Re and the history of reinsurance*, p. 176.

14 An accurate analysis of the question was stated by a contemporary journalist and liberal politician in Salvador Canals i Vilaró (1923), *Cuestiones económicas: el Comité Oficial de Seguros y el reaseguro obligatorio del Estado*, Barcelona, Revista Nuestro Tiempo, p. 2-5, and Pablo Gutiérrez (2014), *El control de divisas durante el primer franquismo. La intervención del reaseguro (1940-1952)*, Madrid, Banco de España.

15 Salvador Canals i Vilaró (1923), *Cuestiones económicas: el Comité Oficial de Seguros y el reaseguro obligatorio del Estado*, p. 12-18.

Table 1. Spanish Reinsurers and the First World War

Company	Representatives	Foundation	Closure	Headquarters
Garantía	Ricardo Palacio	1918	Cont.	Bilbao
Madrid	Alfredo Viliesid	1919	1927	Madrid
Esfera	Enrique Ferrer	1919	1927	Barcelona
Centro Español de Reaseguros	Diego De la Rosa	1919	1933	Madrid
Astur	Manuel Laera	1920	1928	Madrid

Note. Anuario Financiero y de Sociedades Anónimas de España (1921; 1924, 1950-51). *Gaceta de Madrid* for the years of closure. Boletín Oficial de Seguros 1924-1928 for the representatives.

The mode of operation was simple: once the direct link between Spanish insurers and foreign reinsurance networks was interrupted, these companies provided the Committee with market knowledge. Moreover, they served as intermediaries between the state and foreign reinsurance, taking risks from the Committee, retaining a commission and retroceding abroad. In fact, direct insurers and personalities in the financial sphere acquired shares in these companies, which facilitated these contacts: representatives of La Federale, The World Marine & General and Northern Assurance were part of the board of directors of Esfera, while the manager of Centro Español de Reaseguros was linked to Lucero, a marine primary insurer[16].

These reinsurers tried to take advantage of the conditions of reinsurance demand during the First World War, and this circumstantial scope was reflected in their financial foundations. As the marine branch was exempted from capital and reserve requirements included in the regulation passed in 1908, these reinsurers were constituted with extremely low capital resources. One of the most extreme cases was *Astur*, which was registered with a nominal equity value of 200,000 pesetas, of which only 100,000 were actually paid[17].

Within this context, the performance of these companies was closely tied to the survival of the Committee which, in turn, was dependent on the market conditions generated by the First World War. In fact, the competencies of the Committee were partially suspended by decree in August 1920. Until its definitive dissolution in 1924, the Committee's operations were progressively run down. In this scenario, the Spanish reinsurers operated in an intermittent way: *Garantía* announced the end of operations in marine reinsurance in 1922. During the following months, the other

16 Anuario Financiero y de Sociedades Anónimas de España (1924).

17 *Gaceta de Madrid*, 5/10/1925, No. 278, 82.

reinsurers restricted their operations to fire and accident lines. However, the lack of capacity to compete with international reinsurers led to the extinction of these companies: by 1927, only Garantía remained in the market and its business relied not on reinsurance but on direct insurance.

After this process of dissolution of the domestic reinsurance industry and until the Spanish Civil War, there were only two successful initiatives reaching a solid position in the Spanish market. In 1924 the company Castellón Vital was founded in Castellón de la Plana. It operated in all reinsurance branches with moderate profits, but after the Civil War it reoriented the business to direct insurance and changed its name to Compañía Hispanoamericana de Seguros y Reaseguros. The other reinsurer was integrated in La Equitativa (Fundación Rosillo) insurance group. As a part of the group's strategy of growth, the reinsurer was founded in 1928 as a means of capturing a share of a foreign-dominated market.

Analyses the determinants of foreign companies' reinsurance strategies in the Spanish market

As mentioned above, institutional changes in the 1870s and political stability from the 1880s opened the Spanish insurance market to international risk networks. Between 1876 and 1883, fifteen foreign companies were authorised to sell policies in Spain: two from the US, four from the United Kingdom and nine from France. The size of the potential market and the lack of regulatory obstacles contributed to this process. Indeed, the overall economic growth stimulated the demand for insurance, while the first regulation on the performance of foreign insurance companies was not passed until 1893[18]. Despite new regulations, the presence of foreign insurance companies continued to grow during the next two decades. In 1911, after the introduction of the 1908 Insurance Law, fifty-nine foreign offices were registered in Spain[19]. Their incidence was especially intense in life (twelve foreign companies out of a total of nineteen) and fire lines (twenty-nine out of forty-six)[20]. During the 1910s and 1920s, the new trends of economic nationalism, the performance of the markets of origin and the international context of repatriation of capital reduced the relative weight of foreign companies in Spain: the business of foreign life offices reached almost 65% of total premiums in 1918, but it dropped to 38% in 1925; and by 1935, the

18 Tortella *et al.* (2014), *Historia del seguro en España*, p. 112. These data include only Life and Fire branches. The transport branch was not subject to comprehensive legislation and included in the Official Registry until 1920.

19 Frax and Matilla (1996), "Los seguros en España: 1830-1934", p. 199.

20 Tortella *et al.* (2014), *Historia del seguro en España*, p. 112.

total share represented a mere 3.5% of the market[21]. Although the entry and progress of these companies in the Spanish market were subjected to specific market conditions, reinsurance practices played a key role in their development, namely: the use of reinsurance as a way to sound out the market and enter new lines, and the practice of reinsuring risks to their head offices.

According to Raynes (1950) and Wilkins (2009), foreign companies cross borders in three different ways: using local agents, establishing branches and constituting subsidiaries. During the first decades of openness of the Spanish economy, multinationals took the first option due to the lack of maturity of the market. From the 1890s, the establishment of branches became an ordinary practice due to the development of the industry. However, there was a fourth way for companies to indirectly enter the Spanish market: the acceptance of reinsurance premiums underwritten by local companies. In this way, foreign offices got information about features of the market and could take advantage if they eventually established a branch. For instance, in 1847, the British company Alliance got its first contact with the fire business in Spain through a reinsurance treaty signed with the Compagnie Royal d'Assurance, several years before establishing a branch[22].

While this was an unusual practice, foreign companies made wide use of reinsurance once they had settled in the country in order to increase their presence in the market. Indeed, the acceptance of whole or divided portfolios by means of reinsurance was used to extend operations to other lines and to consolidate the position of the offices. Thus, most of the Spanish business of Phoenix Assurance until 1887 was captured as reinsurance premiums ceded by the agency of North British in Malaga. In the same year, the Sun Insurance Office established in Bilbao signed a long-term reinsurance treaty with Alliance that became one of its most important sources of new business[23]. There were not only British companies involved in these practices, but also French and Spanish. In 1908, El Crédito Nacional ceded its whole fire portfolio to the Compagnie Royal d'Assurances, which increased the size of its risk portfolio by almost 20%[24].

These operations were discreetly managed between companies as gentlemen's agreements for decades but, when the first pulses of economic nationalism appeared, they were subject to increasing supervision. In 1901, the French Societé Génerale des Assurance Agricoles et Industrielles agreed to cede 60% of its accident insurance portfolio to the Spanish

21 Tortella *et al.* (2014), *Historia del seguro en España*, 190, and Pons and Gutiérrez (2016), "The actuarial practices of British life insurance companies in peripheral countries: the case of Spain (1890-1936)", p. 9.

22 Pearson (2010), "Las compañías de seguros en España antes de 1914", p. 110.

23 Pearson (2010), "Las compañías de seguros en España antes de 1914", p. 118.

24 Archivo General de la Administración (AGA) (1)26 Caja I-45 Top. 13/31, E-1.

office Hispania[25]. The highly-regulated environment of the branch and the disagreement with state officers about the movement of premiums and reserves attached to policies in force slowed down the process. After two years of negotiations, a new treaty was signed by which the French company ceded the whole portfolio and a share of the constituted reserves[26].

This kind of operation became frequent from the end of the First World War. Indeed, during the 1920s, the withdrawal of several foreign insurance companies was managed through reinsurance treaties. The cession of the New York Life's portfolio to La Equitativa – Fundación Rosillo marked the first milestone in this sequence. The exit of this company entailed the transaction of more than 11% of the life insurance market premiums in Spain, which resulted in new legislation to manage these operations[27]. Similarly, the British Consolidated Assurance left the Spanish market in 1927 by reinsuring its whole life portfolio with the Austrian Phoenix[28]. Even in the 1930s, minor operations of this kind still continued, most of them involving foreign companies leaving the market[29].

Beyond the use of reinsurance as a device to sound out, enter and leave the market, foreign companies displayed quite different quotidian reinsurance strategies. Elements such as the lines in which they operated and the way the company was established in Spain (from local agents or representatives to agencies and even subsidiary companies) contributed to defining these strategies. In fact, actuarial tables used by life insurance companies and the ability to design stable portfolios in the long term made the use of reinsurance as a risk diversification device less necessary in this branch. Quite the opposite, marine and fire lines were the ideal scenario for an intensive use of reinsurance. For the case of fire, Table 2 shows reinsurance indicators of foreign insurance companies operating in Spain between 1908 and 1936, organised by nationality of origin. Even though it is true that the high standard deviation values suggest a high heterogeneity, there are remarkable differences between groups. British and French companies greatly outnumbered the rest of nationalities and both showed reinsurance rate values under

25 AGA (1)26 Caja I-18 Top. 13/31, E-4.

26 The resolution of the case was included in the Royal Order of 9 December 1903, in *Gaceta de Madrid* No. 347, 13/12/1903, p. 944.

27 Pons, "Multinational enterprises and institutional regulation in the life insurance market in Spain 1880-1935", p. 102, analyses the process of withdrawal of the New York and other foreign companies. The new legislation was included in the Royal Decree of 17 March 1922, in *Gaceta de Madrid* No. 77, 18/3/1922, p. 1158.

28 The operation was described by the Official announcement of 25 of March of 1927, in *Gaceta de Madrid* No. 99, 9/4/1927, p. 280, and authorised by the Royal Order 19 May 1927, in *Gaceta de Madrid* No. 142, 22/5/1927, p. 1162.

29 See Pons (2008), "Multinational enterprises and institutional regulation in the life insurance market in Spain 1880-1935" and Pearson (2010), "Las compañías de seguros en España antes de 1914".

30%. On the contrary, Swiss and German companies reinsured more than 50% of their business, with extreme values close to 100%.

Table 2. Mean reinsurance rates in foreign Fire insurance companies in Spain by nationality (1908-1936)

Nationality	No.	% Reinsured	Max.	Min.	Standard Deviation
British	15	15.81	21.79	5.96	16.14
French	10	25.77	37.08	17.55	18.47
Swiss	3	52.98	98.91	42.26	31.30
German	3	62.08	91.39	24.26	28.71

Note. AGA (1) 26 – Cajas I-1 to I-141 Top. 13/31; Comisaría General de Seguros, Memoria sobre las entidades de seguros que operan en España, Years 1911, 1912, 1913 and 1915.

One of the factors that helps explain these differences is the way in which the company chose to establish itself combined with the amount of resources involved in the office's operations in the Spanish market. Indeed, foreign companies opted for different forms of corporate structure to operate in the country: old British and French offices such as Royal Exchange, Sun, Phoenix, L'Urbaine, Du Phenix or L'Abeille began their business in Spain with a single agency but, once integrated into the market, they built wide networks of agents and representatives covering not only Madrid, Barcelona, Bilbao or Malaga, but also other regional markets[30]. Along with this deployment of administrative and human resources, these companies had a strong financial base to face the changing features of the Spanish market and to operate autonomously, but not independently, from their head offices. On the contrary, companies such as La Albingia or Nord Deutsche established their Spanish branches with minimal structures: as many other offices, they began to operate with shared representatives and, once settled in the market, they established one office linked to the cores of the Spanish financial system in Madrid, Barcelona and Bilbao[31]. Mean-

30 For example, in 1911 *L'Urbaine* proudly announced the establishment of 400 agencies in France, Belgium, Netherlands, Spain, Switzerland, Portugal, Egypt and Turkey, emphasizing the density of the Spanish network as proof of its commitment to the development of the insurance market. In a similar way, the advertising of *L'Abeille* highlighted its large reserves deposited in Spain, as much greater than compulsory requirements. *Anuario del comercio, de la industria, de la magistratura y de la administración* (1911: 2275).

31 Though *La Baloise* kept its main office for marine insurance in Barcelona (in San Sebastian from 1932), the fire business was managed by an agent in Madrid shared with the other Swiss company *La Federale*. The case of *Nord Deutsche* is quite similar: the marine branch was operated from Santa Cruz de Tenerife, while the fire line was the responsibility of a single agent in Madrid. In the case of *L'Albinge*, it held a single

while, their financial base relied heavily on the direct support of their mother companies, since they only kept compulsory reserve deposits in Spain. This resulted in a limited underwriting capacity and, usually, in few links with the market[32].

Table 3. Total and internal reinsurance rates in Fire insurance companies in Spain (1926)

Company	Nationality	Agencies in Spain (b)	Reserves in Spain	% Total reinsurance	% Internal reinsurance
L'Abeille	French	12	199,613	2.33	12.34
L'Albinge	German	1	7,060	84.35	76.84
La Baloise	Swiss	1 (1)	230,122	67.05	58.54
La Confiance	French	7	10,021	27.74	–
Guardian Fire	US	6	–	8.21	0
Hispania (a)	Spanish	–	61,357	56.44	87.12
Nord Deutsche	German	1 (1)	12,352	56.74	71.24
Norwich Fire	British	14	179,845	2.11	14.21
Phoenix	British	9	–	3.75	3.95
Sun Insurance	British	12	194,412	10.76	0.98
L'Union	French	8	–	18.46	2.44
Union Assurance	British	6	71,438	14.32	–
L'Urbaine	French	13	395,996	29.12	6.87

Note. AGA (1) 26 – Cajas I-1 to I-12, I-26 to I-51, I-104 to I-128 and I-139, Top. 13/31; Comisaría General de Seguros, Memoria sobre las entidades de seguros que operan en España, Years 1911, 1912, 1913 and 1915.

(a) The data for *Hispania* corresponds to 1916, the last year it was authorised to sell fire insurance. In 1914, it was bought by the Swiss *Zurich*, which accepted most of the portfolio through reinsurance, so we consider this as internal reinsurance.

(b) Shared agencies are included in parentheses.

agency in Bilbao for fire business and another in Seville for marine insurance. See Pons (2002), *Las estrategias de crecimiento de las compañías de seguros en España 1900-1940*, p. 109-100.

32 Although there are few references to the origin of the premiums earned by the companies, most of the 50% of the business written by *L'Albinge*, *La Baloise* and *Nord Deutsche* in the period 1925-1930 were premiums accepted from *La Unión y el Fénix Español*, *La Catalana* and other major Spanish companies. AGA (1) 26 Cajas I-12 Top. 13/31 E-6, I-28 Top. 13/31 E-4, I-96 Top. 13/31 E-2.

Table 3 shows the main features of a sample of foreign companies selling fire policies in Spain, including the number of exclusive agencies, ongoing reserves deposited in Spain, total premiums reinsured and the share of reinsurance ceded to the head offices in the country of origin. As shown, British and French companies kept a wider network of agencies and larger reserves in Spain than Swiss or German ones, with the exception of La Confiance and La Baloise. At the same time, reinsurance rates show that German and Swiss insurers were more prone to purchase reinsurance than large French and British offices. Moreover, while the share of reinsurance ceded to its head office reached a maximum of 14% for Norwich Fire, the companies La Baloise, Nord Deutsche and L'Albinge all reinsured more than half of the business written to their country of origin.

In fact, while Royal Exchange and L'Abeille branches retained between 85 and 95% of the direct business underwritten, La Baloise and La Albingia kept only between 5 and 10%, reinsuring large amounts of risks to their head offices. These were not isolated cases. According to the data, it could be stated that well-established companies from the United Kingdom and France made an intensive use of financial and management resources to manage the branch as an autonomous office. The high level of reserves deposited in Spain and the support of several regional agencies provided long-term scope, while maintaining access to capital funding sources in the country of origin. In parallel, several companies, especially German and Swiss ones, were operating as bridgeheads for their head offices, using a minimal corporate structure to take risks in the Spanish market and channel the business directly to their countries of origin.

Far from being a key determinant, these features of reinsurance practices were related to the different business strategies of foreign companies. Structural diversity among foreign companies connects directly with the different theoretical approaches to reinsurance. In fact, reinsurance works as a risk diversification device for insurance companies. From this perspective, companies try to reduce the volatility of risks within the business portfolio by using reinsurance in a limited way, since the main goal is to retain a balanced pool of risks[33]. This traditional way of using reinsurance seems to have been the main component of British and French firms operating in Spain, since their reinsurance purchases were made for a limited amount and outside the company's group (see Table 3). As a consequence, it would indicate a reinsurance strategy based on actuarial criteria, aimed at mitigating underwriting risks on the basis of claims experience.

33 Gerathewohl (1993), *Reaseguro. Teoría y Práctica.* According to risk theory, optimisation of the portfolio would be reached when the claim experience of the business written is equal to the claim experience of the business reinsured.

From another perspective, reinsurance works as an imperfect substitute for capital within ruin theory. Indeed, insurers facing a lack of financial support purchase reinsurance as a way to enhance their underwriting capacity without increasing equity capital[34]. In the case of Swiss and German companies, they usually had less financial and management resources and higher rates of purchase of reinsurance services. Moreover, a significant share of the reinsured premiums of these companies was ceded to their head offices, that is, internal reinsurance. As a result, this would indicate the reinsurance strategy as a financial decision, rather than an actuarial one.

In spite of these differences, both approaches resulted in a similar macroeconomic performance. The Spanish insurance industry got additional underwriting capacity to cover more risks by means of using foreign capital, either by direct investment made by foreign companies in the country or by an intensive practice of purchasing reinsurance abroad. However, they display two different forms of internationalisation: while in the first case this implied the slow implementation of large amounts of financial and management resources, in the second this was reduced to a minimum level through an extensive use of alternate financial devices such as reinsurance.

The uses of reinsurance by domestic companies and the links with internationalisation and growth strategies

Reinsurance practice among Spanish companies was not very different from the strategy of the multinationals. It fluctuated between a technical resource and a lucrative business. Among this group there were, exceptionally, companies or mutual societies of local or regional scope and with limited business. There were no such companies among the multinationals as they had to have exceeded this scale in their domestic market in order to expand abroad. Furthermore, the private insurance law of 1908, the first specific legislation for the sector in Spanish economic history, did not regulate reinsurance activity. This lack of legislation and control is reflected in the lack of official aggregate data on reinsurance between 1908 and 1940. Therefore, as mentioned above, in order to analyse this activity, it has been necessary to resort to the companies' actual balance

34 See, for example, Mayers and Smith (1990), "On the corporate demand for insurance: evidence from the reinsurance market", Powell and Somner (2007), "Internal versus external capital markets in the insurance industry: The role of insurance", and Deelstra and Plantin (2014), *Risk theory and reinsurance*.

sheets or the information declared on reinsurance in specific lines such as fire or transport.

Likewise, this absence of regulation of the reinsurance business allowed insurance companies to reinsure in lines in which they did not operate in direct insurance, which provided additional lucrative business. The first legislation on commercial reinsurance operations in Spain was not introduced until the decree of 29 September 1944. This decree established that only specifically authorised companies could reinsure. Foreign companies authorised by the *Dirección General de Seguros* (Directorate General of Insurance) and general insurance companies could only carry out reinsurance operations in those lines in which they were authorised to practice direct insurance in.

This prohibition put an end to a practice that was very widespread among Spanish insurance companies from 1880 to 1944, by means of which reinsurance operations were carried out not only for technical reasons such as risk diversification but also as part of a lucrative supplementary business. To document this mode of reinsurance it is necessary to resort to the minutes of the General Meetings of some companies and their balance sheets, as these items did not appear in insurance statistics. This practice was documented in the Banco Vitalicio de España, which operated in life insurance from its constitution but also, from at least 1918, signed reinsurance contracts in the fire branch that, as commented in the Annual General Meeting, '*continue to produce satisfactory results*'[35]. With time this practice was extended successfully, and '*the other branches where we are dealing exclusively in reinsurance have also produced satisfactory results*'[36].

In some cases, reinsurance operations in a particular branch led to procuring contracts in direct insurance in the medium term. Prior to 1920, the Banco Vitalicio de España represented other companies in transport insurance. In this year, it decided to operate in the transport branch in direct insurance and, by extension, in reinsurance, thereby taking advantage of the Royal Decree of 13 August 1920. This regulation obliged companies operating in transport insurance to apply for inclusion in the official registry established by the Law of 14 May 1908. This immediately resulted in a dramatic transformation of the branch. This obligation entailed a substantial change in the business due to the new requirements established by the Administration (deposits, reserves and declaration of premiums). A considerable number of foreign companies that operated with total freedom and little taxation abandoned the Spanish market and

35 Banco Vitalicio de España. Minutes of the AGM of 7 May 1919.

36 Banco Vitalicio de España. Minutes of the AGM of 27 May 1924.

some national companies wound up their business[37]. However, for the *Banco Vitalicio de España* it was the starting point of its diversification strategy. It increased its offer on the basis of an intensive use of reinsurance, which enabled an increase in the scale of operations without increasing its capital and without unduly raising risk. The Board of Directors, however, also contemplated another objective, which was participation in the international reinsurance market:

> The reinsurance of our surplus is all with top companies, which will allow us to extend our field of action enormously, as we have obtained important reciprocal cessions[38].

Thus, the Banco Vitalicio de España did not reinsure its operations with the sole aim of increasing the scale of subscriptions to make up for its lack of capital, or of diversifying risk by ceding part of its premiums, but also to participate in the reinsurance market by obtaining reciprocal cessions, that is, collecting premiums as compensation for business ceded. In this branch, the company started a strategy of reinsurance cessions of between 50 and 70% of premiums (see Table 4). Nevertheless, the results of this practice led to this figure increasing until it exceeded 80% between 1928 and 1935. This ensured a margin of profit, or rather a commission, of around 15%, which was added to the premiums collected as risk acceptance in the reinsurance market.

Table 4. Percentage of premiums the Banco Vitalicio de España ceded in reinsurance in the transport branch (thousands of pesetas)

	Premiums collected	Premiums reinsured	Reinsurance as % of total premiums	Claims	Claims borne by reinsurers and %	
1922	992	691	69.6	451	309	68.5
1923	1,560	1,161	74.4	683	543	79.5
1924	2,601	1,415	54.4	1,136	715	62.9
1925	2,749	1,397	50.8	1,854	905	48.7
1926	3,240	1,895	58.4	2,793	1,668	59.7
1927	2,490	1,882	75.5	1,794	1,279	71.3
1928	2,324	1,873	80.5	1,311	1,052	80.2
1929	2,864	2,381	83.1	1,571	1,367	86.9

37 Jerònia Pons (2003), "Diversificación y cartelización en el seguro español, 1914-1935", *Revista de Historia Económica*, 21, p. 573.

38 Banco Vitalicio de España. Minutes of the AGM of 27 May 1924.

	Premiums collected	Premiums reinsured	Reinsurance as % of total premiums	Claims	Claims borne by reinsurers and %	
1930	2,703	2,187	80.9	1,424	1,223	85.8
1931	1,840	1,510	82.0	903	775	85.7
1932	2,730	2,356	86.2	2,129	1,964	92.2
1933	3,187	2,752	86.3	2,004	1,851	92.3
1934	3,396	2,870	84.4	1,576	1,335	84.6
1935	3,141	2,629	83.7	1,161	1,001	86.2

Note. Minutes of the AGM of the Banco Vitalicio de España. Generalli historical archive.

Nevertheless, these practices were not exclusive to the transport branch. A medium-term analysis of the Spanish companies in the fire branch, from 1912 to 1931, shows that national insurers, as in the case of the multinationals, did not have a homogeneous reinsurance strategy. The percentage of reinsured premiums can be explained according to different strategies and interests. On the one hand, as with the multinationals, the reinsurance contract was the most used formula when it came to entering or withdrawing from the branch. In Table 5 it can be seen how El Norte (which ceased operating in this branch in 1915), La Alianza de Santander (1927) and La Mundial Agraria (1930) applied this solution.

Generally speaking, the heterogeneity of reinsurance practices within the group of national companies operating in this branch can be seen (Table 5). In accordance with previous literature, an initial hypothesis could suggest a classification depending on the type of company and organisational form[39]. The mutual societies, due to their lack of share capital, were more inclined to use reinsurance to expand their operations without jeopardising their financial stability[40]. However, this mechanism is not the same in all the mutuals in the cases analysed. Whereas the Mutua General de Seguros and La Mutual Franco Española ceded business to reinsurance at a rate of over 70%, La Mutual Agraria scarcely reinsured 30% of premiums collected. If we add the small mutual societies against fire in the provincial capitals and small cities, such as those in Valladolid,

39 Robin Pearson (2015), "The development of reinsurance markets in Europe during the nineteenth century", Lilljegren and Andersson, "Variation in organizational form across lines of property insurance: Sweden, 1913-1939" and Robin Pearson and Takau Yoneyama, *Corporate Forms and Organizational Choice in International Insurance*, Oxford, Oxford University Press.

40 Pablo Gutiérrez and Jerònia Pons (2016), "Risk management and reinsurance strategies in the Spanish insurance market (1880-1940)", *Business History*.

Albacete and Carmona, to the sample, the heterogeneity is even greater[41]. In this respect, elements such as the scope of the mutuals' operations, whether at local, regional or national level, and the competition present in the market, seem to be determining factors in the reinsurance strategies of these societies.

Leaving to one side the criterion of organisational form, two groups can clearly be distinguished among the fire insurance companies. In one group would be the companies that during the period under study rarely exceeded 50% of premiums reinsured: Alianza de Santander, La Aurora, Celtiberia, La Estrella, Hispania, La Patria Hispana and La Previsión Nacional. In the second group would be the insurance companies and mutuals that resorted to reinsurance to a greater extent, with cession rates in excess of 50% and, in general, over 70%: la Equitativa (Fundación Rosillo), La Unión y El Fénix Español, Mutua General de Seguros and La Mutua Franco Española.

Among the first, the lesser use of reinsurance in their operations was due to various factors in common: the scale of their operations at regional level and the homogeneity of their risks. Moreover, there was a third differentiating factor: these were companies and mutuals specialised in a single branch, which made their risk portfolio more uniform. This was the case of companies such as Previsión Nacional, Previsión Española, Aurora and Celtiberia which, except some isolated incursion into the transport branch, maintained the fire branch as their main source of business. A prime example of this was La Sociedad Catalana de Seguros de Incendios, which continued as a company specialised in the fire branch and increased in scale thanks to the purchase of a large number of portfolios from companies that abandoned the branch. It acquired the fire portfolio of Hispania in 1916, when this company was taken over by the Swiss Zurich[42] and concentrated its activities in the accident branch; and in 1921 it acquired the portfolio of Celtiberia after its liquidation[43].

Nevertheless, there are also exceptions in this group, such as the case of La Estrella. This insurer was founded in Cartagena on 7 June 1901 by the Banco de Cartagena, which subscribed for 18,000 of the 20,000 shares issued. From 1912 it operated in the branches of fire, life, industrial and individual accidents, and in the transport branch from 1923. However, from its very foundation this company was linked with a banking group,

41 Gutiérrez and Pons (2016), "Risk management and reinsurance strategies in the Spanish insurance market (1880-1940)".

42 Jerònia Pons (2016), *130 años de promesas cumplidas. Grupo Zurich en España*, Barcelona, Editorial Planeta.

43 Jerònia Pons (2002), p. 55.

over time the Banco Hispano Americano, and thus had external capital which backed its diversification and the increase in scale of its operations.

In the second group, comprising companies with high rates of cession of risks to reinsurance, there are both mutuals and large joint-stock companies, each with different motivations. Thus, on the one hand we find the Mutual Franco-Española and the Mutua General de Seguros, which resorted to the reinsurance market more as a financial mechanism than as an actuarial tool of the risk portfolios. Indeed, these mutuals used reinsurance both to increase the scale of their operations and to diversify their business, thereby minimising the financial risks. In a nutshell, they sought to increase their presence in the market, overcoming the lack of share capital by means of recourse to reinsurance, as reflected in the literature on reinsurance[44]. The other part of the group was made up of large insurers such as La Unión y El Fénix Español, La Equitativa (Fundación Rosillo) and the Banco Aragonés. All three of these were large-scale operators, which occupied leading positions in most of the lines they operated in and were in direct contact with the international reinsurance market. This capacity to access the international circuits of risk exchange determined their high rates of cession of risks to a large extent: the possibility of accessing more competitive and developed reinsurance markets, along with the ability to capture foreign risks, made this tool an ideal mechanism for both modelling their risk portfolios and for obtaining alternative means of financing.

From the outset, La Unión y El Fénix Español functioned as a structure with two headquarters: one in Madrid for direct insurance business and another in Paris where it concentrated its reinsurance activity and, through which, it channelled its reinsurance operations that even went beyond European borders[45]. La Equitativa (Fundación Rosillo) was founded in 1916 by the former agents of the Equitable Life in Spain. The company decided to start operating in the fire branch in 1923, and in 1928, instead of continuing to diversify, it was decided to create two new companies. On the one hand, La Equitativa (Fundación Rosillo, riesgos generales) was constituted with a capital of 5 million pesetas to provide insurance in the branches of fire, accidents, transport and theft. On the other hand, a reinsurer was founded with a capital of 10 million pesetas.

44 Gerathewohl (1993), *Reaseguro. Teoría y práctica*, y Pearson (1995), "The development of reinsurance markets in Europe during the nineteenth century".

45 Gutiérrez and Pons (2016), "Risk management and reinsurance strategies in the Spanish insurance market (1880-1940)".

Table 5. Percentage of premiums ceded in reinsurance by Spanish insurers in the fire branch (1912-1931)

	1912	1913	1914	1915	1916	1917	1918	1919	1920	1921	1922	1923	1924	1925	1926	1927	1928	1929	1930	1931
JOINT-STOCK COMPANIES																				
La Alianza de Santander	56.8	53.3	51.4	53.7	53.7	57.4	60.0	56.4	49.8	63.7	51.8	49.2	41.6	55.0	66.3	100	100	100	100	
Aurora	38.3	32.9	33.2	31.7	30.2	40.4	52.7	42.3	40.1	41.5	40.5	40.9	42.5	43.8	42.9	44.1	44.9	47.9		
Banco Aragonés	60.5	66.6	58.4	59.4	60.2	47.8	44.3	47.5	41.3	37.4	38.9	40.1	41.8	39.7	39.7	46.4	75.8	78.7	76.0	
La Catalana	22.4	23.0	24.5	32.4	28.1	73.8	39.8	44.1	46.0	54.8	56.8	63.5	61.3	61.3	56.7	66.1	65.2	65.1	63.1	
Celtiberia	32.1	35.7	37.0	37.2	37.5	39.0	40.1	50.9	55.5	63.9										
La Equitativa (Fundación Rosillo)												65.9	74.6	81.3	86.8	76.0	79.3	64.8	72.9	81.0
La Estrella	19.9	22.7	21.6	18.7	24.5	23.0	25.2	21.2	24.0	23.9	23.5	24.1	23.4	22.1	20.2	19.6	16.2	15.8	14.4	16.3
Hispania	26.7	21.6	27.6	42.5	56.4	34.8														
El Norte	40.4	37.2	37.2	16.6	100	100	100							50.8	48.5	56.3	57.9	58.0	54.7	54.3
La Patria Hispana									22.4	19.4	22.2	18.5	17.7	18.6	21.4	22.8	22.7	25.3	22.1	19.3
La Previsión Española	3.5	3.56	4.5	6.8	9.07	9.4	12.4	13.7	14.9	14.1	14.7	16.5	18.7	19.3	18.7	20.1	19.2	21.0	23.0	24.8
La Previsión Nacional	17.7	19.5	20.8	21.0	13.7	18.8	20.0	15.1												
La Unión y el Fénix Español	72.1	78.0	65.6	75.2	69.6	69.0	68.7	69.6	61.8	60.2	74.0	67.7	71.2	75.3	51.4		62.2	64.5	54.4	52.6
MUTUAS																				
La Mundial Agraria									33.5	37.9	33.6	31.6	32.5	34.1	32.4	32.6	26.5		99.9	
Mutua General de Seguros																72.1	81.8	92.8	85.7	92.0
La Mutual Franco Española									79.2	68.0	83.1	78.7	79.3	84.2	87.5	81.9	87.2	85.2	87.1	99.5

Note. AGA (1) 26 – Cajas I-1 to I-141 Top. 13/31; Comisaría General de Seguros, Memoria sobre las entidades de seguros que operan en España, Years 1911, 1912, 1913 and 1915.

Although the two companies were legally independent they acted as a group with a common strategy. The diversification initiated in the fire branch in 1923 was achieved through an intensive use of reinsurance: the cession of risks reached over 60% of the risks contracted. Moreover, this figure increased from 1928 onwards as it included the retrocession of risks captured in both the national and international markets to its subsidiary (Table 5).

Finally, it is documented that the Banco Aragonés, the same as La Unión y el Fénix Español, had an agency in Paris. This office was geared to the selection and capture of risks of different branches for reinsurance from the beginning of the First World War. Once this activity was consolidated, in 1924, reinsurance premiums were worth more than five million pesetas, while the direct insurance operations in the fire branch were worth slightly more 900,000 pesetas in the same year[46]. In this respect, the company had specialised in this type of operations: after the war, the company's restructuring efforts focused on a recovery plan that would allow reinsurance activity to continue. This activity, in the words of internal reports, "*is one of the main manifestations of our corporate activity*". Its high level of reinsurance in the fire branch, therefore, was not exclusively due to technical factors or the actuarial design of its portfolio, but also to its participation as a reinsurer in the cession, acceptance and retrocession of risks. In fact, reinsurance was its main line of insurance business.

Conclusion

In spite of Spain's relative actuarial and financial backwardness and the immature management of its insurance business, modern techniques such as reinsurance were widely practised from the late 19th century. Both in the traditional branches of marine and fire insurance and in the new lines of life and accident insurance foreign companies, national stock companies and mutuals resorted to this tool both to win new business and to balance their risk portfolios.

However, its widespread use in Spain did not lead to the creation of pure reinsurers, over and above the ephemeral experiences linked to demand of the First World War. This lack of pure reinsurers was not an obstacle to the development of this activity, largely because the big Spanish direct insurance companies assumed the leadership role in reinsurance in

46 Banco Aragonés de Seguros y Crédito. Report read at the ordinary General Shareholders' Meeting held on 18 April 1925, Zaragoza (1925, p. 7). The reinsurance claims paid were for a total of 3,326,688.19 pesetas.

Spain, while at the same time connecting with the international reinsurance flows.

The diversity of reinsurance strategies was linked to the different modes and functions of reinsurance. The use of reinsurance for both technical operations and those with a purely financial goal gave rise to a heterogeneous set of causes for the reinsurance practices of both foreign and national companies. Indeed, those factors indicated by theory as determinants in the demand for reinsurance are recorded in documents in the case of the Spanish market. The corporate form certainly influenced reinsurance practice, as did the availability of financial resources. Nevertheless, there are several nuances in this market linked to diversification to new branches, the scale of operations and especially, at times, the high level of reinsurance of large companies due to their participation in the international reinsurance market.

The Development of Spanish Reinsurance from 1940 to the Present Day

Leonardo Caruana de las Cagigas

The world reinsurance market in the 1960s and 1970s

The reinsurance market in Western Europe and the United States changed between 1965 and 1975, as shown in Table 1. In 1965, Western European countries had 66.7% of premiums, the United States 24.7% and other countries 8.6%. Ten years later, in 1975, Western European countries had 61.3%, the United States 22% and other regions 16.7%. While the percentage doubled in other countries, in Western Europe and the United States it dropped by 5.4 points and 2.7 points, respectively. However, the reinsurance companies are mainly German, Swiss, American, French or British. The main companies are from these countries: Munich Re ($2,147 m), Swiss Re ($1,467 m), General Re ($566 m), SCOR ($407 m), Mercantile and General Group ($342 m).[1]

Table 1. Insurance premiums and reinsurance premiums in 1965 and 1975

	Western Europe		United States		Others*	
Year	$ billions	%	$ billions	%	$ billions	%
1965	10.8/3.7	34.4	25.3/1.4	5.5	3.5/0.5	13.6
1975	39.5/11.4	28.9	66.2/4.1	6.2	18.4/3.1	16.9

*Mainly Japan, Canada and Australia.
Source: *Sigma* 2 (Feb. 1977), p. 10.

It is worth noting that few companies dominate the global reinsurance market. In 1975, there were 191 companies, of which the top fifteen had over 50% of the reinsurance premiums and the top 58 companies had 86%. Euro-

1 International Insurance Monitor 1979.

pean and American companies accounted for 85.6% of premium income.[2] In addition, many companies were subsidiaries of foreign companies (42 companies), insurance groups (81) and pure reinsurers (32), which were responsible for legal cessions, particularly in developing countries.[3] Finally, London was the financial centre of the reinsurance market in the 1970s. In the City in 1976, the financial institutions' earnings amounted to £1,540 m and the insurance business to £606 m that can be divide in £174 m from companies, £279 m from Lloyd's and £154 million from brokers.[4]

Insurance in developing countries

In the 1960s–1970s, the great majority of the population in developing countries could not pay an insurance premium. The insurance sector was developed by foreign insurance companies which belonged to the British or French empire or industrialized countries such as the United States and Germany. For these developing countries, London was the most important centre, since there was no local financial capability and there were few regulations. Nevertheless, this changed in some countries.

When some countries achieved independence, they developed statutory insurance regulations with the purpose to achieve capability in the field of insurance: "Legal frameworks for insurance introduced in most developing countries over the past three decades reduced the degree of predominance of foreign insurance in these markets."[5] The reason for this reduction was the requirement of registration formalities, deposit funds, compulsory local reserves, etc. As a result, foreign companies stopped operating in those countries unless they had large portfolios or held a stake in a local company, which could become a holding. The foreign companies provided capital, management capability and training capacity instead of a reinsurance placement.

The decrease in the number of foreign insurance companies in many countries led to the creation of local companies that would fill the gap. In this process, many restrictions were imposed on foreign insurers, which in some cases were prevented from operating. In other countries, a government insurance monopoly was created. If the government was more

2 Pierre De Vogüe, P. (1977), "Professional Reinsurance and the Problem of Developing Countries", First Third World Insurance Congress, Manila, p. 88.

3 Pierre De Vogüe, P. (1977), "Professional Reinsurance and the Problem of Developing Countries", First Third World Insurance Congress, Manila, p. 90.

4 L'Argus International (1978), p. 112.

5 United Nations (1980), *Transnational Reinsurance Operations*, UN. New York, United Nations Centre on Transnational Corporations, 26.

liberal, the foreign company was subject to financial requirements and control of their remittances abroad.

Thanks to this policy, an insurance sector was created and consolidated in many developing countries. Foreign companies eventually became the major supplier of insurance cover in the home market. However, the insurance sector in this period saw a reduction in business due to the lack of local investors because of the long-term nature of its profitability. Consequently, the insurance sector shrank considerably. Thus, in Latin America they were 886 companies in 1975 vs 1,015 companies in 1968, whereas in developed countries, there were 18 companies for every million people and in developing countries only 3.

The development of reinsurance companies 1940–2015

The development of the reinsurance market in Spain is far more complex and was the culmination of the so-called take off.[6] How did the country manage to take off? As regards reinsurance, when Spanish companies were able to compete successfully in the global market?

The Spanish Industrial Revolution took place between 1950 and 1980. It is convenient to mention three significant changes in the currency, the financial system and reinsurance. First, the Spanish currency (*peseta*) followed the IMF criteria in the 1960s. Second, a modern and reliable financial system and a reliable stock market were functioning and the state regularly paid the interest of its debt. Third, the reinsurance sector developed, as we shall explain in the remainder of the chapter.

In the 1950–1980 period, Spain became an industrialized country, although it still had some characteristics of underdeveloped countries. Thus, there were very few reinsurance companies able to develop the business successfully because they lacked the economic capability that requires know-how and sufficient capital. As in other emerging countries, the Spanish insurance market was heavily dependent on foreign reinsurance, though not as heavily as some islands in the Atlantic or in the Pacific.[7] The foreign companies controlled assets, covered risk, and had a great spread that minimized risk.

In Spain, the reinsurance market under the Franco regime developed with excessive government control and strong restriction for the foreign

6 Walt W. Rostow (1960), "The Five Stages of Growth – A Summary", *The Stages of Economic Growth: A Non-Communist Manifesto*, Cambridge, Cambridge University Press, pp.. 4–16.

7 UN Report 1980, pp. 28, 51.

companies. The theory behind this idea was the autarky policy. They had the belief that Spanish companies can do it better than foreign companies can. There was a strong nationalist thought in those days. This was not new, in the interwar period there was a solid protectionist policy for example "The Equitable life" left Spain in 1916 as has been explain in the last chapter. Anyway, it was far more passionate and irrational these ideas in the 1940s. They did consider that it would be more beneficial for the economy of the country if Spanish firms managed all reinsurance (see list of companies in 1949 in reinsurance in the Appendix, Table 2 and the graphic with the change from 1949 to 1959).

At the beginning of the 1940s was a terrible moment because the civil war disrupted substantially the financial situation in the country. Spanish reinsurance companies before the war were only two companies: Garantía, S.A. de Reaseguros with its headquarters in Bilbao, founded in 1918, with 2,000,000 pesetas of nominal capital in 1943 and La Equitativa (F. R.) Reaseguros with its headquarters in Madrid, founded in 1928 with a nominal capital of 10,000,000 pesetas in 1943. The first started reinsurance of life in 1936, only 3 months before the Spanish Civil War, very risky moment and reinsurance of Transport during the Second World War, in 1940. Clearly, the members of the board of directors were brave people. It was a captive reinsurance company of the insurance company Aurora, also with its headquarters in Bilbao. In 1950, they had in the board of directors Emilio Botín of Bank Santander and the brother of Franco, Nicolás Franco Bahamonde, the President and General Director was Fermín Rosillo.

From 1940 to 1989, they will appear 19 pure reinsurance companies with very different stories each one. From the company like "Cresa" founded in Barcelona as a reinsurance company name: Cresa, Compañía Anónima de Reaseguros, S.A. officially recognize by the Spanish administration since 23 July 1941. Some legal modification was incorporated and was definitely recognized since 10 December 1941.[8] This company was authorized to develop the business of reinsurance in all type of reinsurance except life reinsurance. However, five years later in the General Assembly of the company, 20 February 1945, they decided to cancel all the reinsurance and started with life insurance, fire insurance and individual accident insurance. So, it was really a short story in reinsurance. Lastly, they change the headquarters from Barcelona to Madrid in 1956.

Another company was the opposite: it started with direct insurance and eventually developed only reinsurance business. This company was Compañía Mediterránea de Seguros y Reaseguros, S.A. with its central office in Barcelona was legally accepted by the official registration of insur-

8 *Boletín Oficial del Estado* No. 361, of 27/12/1941, pp. 10, 132.

ance companies on 21 August 1942, developing the business in both direct insurance and reinsurance in Fire insurance, robbery insurance, civil responsibility insurance and transport insurance. In addition, this company the next year was authorized to sign premiums in life reinsurance on 22 September 1943. The President was Luis Puig de la Bellacasa y Deu, General Director was Juan Antonio Parpal Bruna. It started with 2,000,000 pesetas of registered capital or nominal capita, which increased to 5,000,000 in 1950.

With this company, in the long run the reinsurance business did go far better, because four years later, on 6 November 1947, they made a big change. They ask at the Administration to cancel the authorization to operate in direct insurance. In addition, they received authorization to develop all types of reinsurance. Finally, they even change the name of the company to Compañia Mediterránea de Reaseguros, obviously to make it clear to all the clients or the new possible clients what was there business.

Other companies will be relevant but last for a short time for example: Compañía General de Reaseguros founded in Barcelona in 1942 and will last until 1959. Register capital 5,000,000 pesetas, President, Juan Antonio Gamazo y de Abarca, Count of Gamazo, between the board there was a famous Spanish lawyer Joaquín Garrigues Diaz Cañabate.

We must follow with other pure reinsurance companies. The common factor they all disappear before the end of the century. These companies are 13: Consorcio Español de Reaseguradores; Reaseguradora Española, S.A.; Compañía Española de Reaseguros; Nervión Reaseguros S.A.; Guipuzcoa S.A. Reaseguros; Centro Levantino de Reaseguro; Continental Compañía Española de Reaseguros; Compañía Ibérica de Reaseguros, S.A.; Goya, Hispano-Inglesa de Reaseguros, S.A.; Reaseguradora Colon, Albatros Reaseguros, Reunisa and Ocaso Reaseguros.[9]

The first, Consorcio Español de Reaseguros, S.A. (CERSA), started in Seville in 1939, nominal capital 10,000,000 pesetas that paid out 3,000,000 pesetas in 1950. Authorized on 12 April 1940 to develop all type of reinsurance except life reinsurance and, on 16 December 1943, also life reinsurance. President Juan Borges Fe, General Director Francisco Reyes Aldave and Chief Executive Officer Juan Cantalapiedra Fernández de Toledo. This company will change its name to Sociedad Anónima Española de Reaseguros Nacionales e Internacionales (SAERNI) on 18 April 1961, and city to Barcelona. However, the company will have a short life; it will be absorbed in 1978 by the company Iberia, Compañía Anónima de Seguros Generales. The President and General Director of

---

9 Jerònia Pons (2012), "Spain: International Influence on the Domestic Insurance MarKet", *World Insurance*, ed. Borscheid and Haueter, Oxford, Oxford University Press, p. 202.

both companies was Juan Rosell Esmet. This last company ended in the CLEA on 11 March 1998.[10]

The CLEA (*Comisión Liquidadora de Entidades Aseguradoras*) is an important system created in Spain in 1984 by the Government to solve the difficulties that many companies had by a Royal Decret Law 10/1984, 11 June as urgent measures. In fact, this government office was improvised by the few people that were at the beginning and will have several legislation problems that will end in the Spanish Supreme Court. From the first moment, they had many insurance companies that were in the CLEA because they were bankrupt. The purpose behind the office was that the clients should not suffer the problem of these companies. In 1984, they were in the list of the CLEA 14 insurance companies that were bankrupt or close to be bankrupt. Between 1984 and 2000 more than 200 insurance companies will be manage by the CLEA. The crisis of 1973 followed with another in 1979 hit nasty to banks, insurance companies and all types of companies in Spain. The insurance companies stood in favour of this substantial improvement for the general interest of the insurance services and all paid with each premium a percentage for the general benefit of the service offer by the insurance companies manage by the CLEA. With this money that they paid to the clients of the insurance companies bankrupt, also sort out a solution for the workers of the companies that close and the suppliers. This official office was run by the state and it end in the Consorcio de Compensación de Seguros in 2002 that is also a public institution.

The second company, Reaseguradora Española, S.A. (RESA), authorized 8 March 1940, was a captive company of Bilbao Compañía Anónima de Seguros founded in 1920, both with the headquarters in Bilbao. They increased the reinsurance business three years later with life reinsurance on 31 March 1943. The President was José Galiano y Bengoechea, Chief Executive Officer was José María Soroa y Reyes and General Director was José Miguel Soroa y Gómez. This company changed its activities and name after 30 December 1966; the new name was Seguros Orbita, S.A. Practically thirty years later, the whole portfolio will pass to Bilbao Compañía Anónima de Seguros y Reaseguros, and the company cancelled on 30 December 1995.[11]

The third, Compañía Española de Reaseguros (C.E.R.), was from Madrid; legally recognized 14 January 1941, to do all type of reinsurance and nominal capital was 12,000,000 pesetas. President Ernesto Anastasio Pascual and Delegate administrate Luis Hermida Higueras. This company was the captive reinsurance company of La Unión y El Fénix Española. One of the most important insurance companies in Spain up to 1990s. Founded in 1864, that

[10] Document BOE-A-1998-6162.
[11] Document BOE-A-1996-3894.

had an important participation of Banesto. However, the origin of this bank was the French company, Sociedad General de Crédito Mobiliario Español founded in 1856 by the well-known Isaac Pereire. Finally, was cancelled from the special registration of insurance companies on 3 November 1995.[12]

Fourth, Nervion Reaseguros, started 14 February 1941 in the well-known street of Arenal in Bilbao for all type of reinsurance. It had as nominal capital 5,000,000 pesetas, President Alvaro Areitio Zabala and was the captive company of the insurance company La Polar founded in April 1901, which was linked with the Banco Bilbao, in fact, four of the board of directors were of the Bank. This company will be bought by MAPFRE in 1981 and it was name Mapfre Reaseguros.

The next Spanish reinsurance company, fifth, was Company Guipuzcoa Reaseguros, S.A., from the city of San Sebastián, that started on 11 March 1941, was authorized for all type of reinsurance, except life reinsurance. Two years later, on 9 June 1943, it was authorized in life reinsurance that the Extraordinary General Assembly of the company demanded a year previously, in May 1942. Nominal capital was 2,000,000 pesetas that will increase up to 5,000,000 pesetas in 1968. President Julian Lojendrio Garin and General Directors were Federico Garsa and Francisco Civeti. This company was the captive company of Compañía Vascongada de Seguros y Reaseguros, founded 7 April 1930. The Company Guipuzcoa Reaseguros, S.A. will be eliminated from the official registration of insurance companies on 21 November 1989 and become extinct.[13]

We follow with Centro Levantino de Reaseguro, S.A. a captive company of Union Levantina S.A. de Seguros, founded in 1924 from Valencia. The president was José García Sanfelix, the manager director José Luis Cardenas Giménez will be authorized 7 January 1942 in all type of reinsurance except life reinsurance, nominal capital was 5,000,000 pesetas and pay out 3,200,000 in 1950. In 1943, they change the name to Centro Levantino de Seguros y Reaseguros, S.A. because they were authorized for maritime insurance. It was eliminated from the official registration of insurance companies the 2 January 1987 and extinct.[14]

The next company, Continental Compañía Española de Reaseguros, had administrative authorization on 10 February 1943 for all type of reinsurance, nominal capital 10,000,000 pesetas, pay out 5,000,000 in 1950 and in 1968 will be 17,000,000 pesetas. The head office was in Madrid. President Manuel Arias-Dávila Manzanos, Count of Puñonrostro and the Manager Director was Rafael Linage Zaldívar. This company will be a captive company of Prevision Española founded in 1883 in Seville. It

12 Document BOE-A-1995-26041.

13 Document BOE-A-1990-1427.

14 Document BOE-A-1987-3548.

was eliminated from the official registration of insurance companies on 26 December 1989 and put into compulsory liquidation.[15]

Another company will change its name twice: first was La Equitativa Hispano Americana with its headquarters in Madrid. Founded in 1944, that will develop reinsurance since 1948, which change the name in 1958 in the official documents as Compañia Ibero Americana de Reaseguros, S.A. but again it will change the name to Compañia Ibérica de Reaseguros, S.A. nominal capital 25,000,000 pesetas, which was the captive reinsurance company of La Equitativa S.A. The President was Antonio Botella García and Juan José Rosillo Martos was in the board of directors, in 1970 the President was Antonio Rosillo Herrero and Rafael Rosillo Herrero vice-president. It was eliminated from the official registration of insurance companies on 26 May 1997 and became extinct.[16]

We follow with Goya, Hispano-Inglesa de Reaseguros, S.A. it will be the leader in reinsurance companies in Spain in the early years of the 1970s with an important nominal capital of 25,000,000 pesetas. It had an important development out of Spain, especially in Latin America. This was relatable new strategy for the Spanish companies an especially for reinsurance. Unfortunately, it will have a short development.

The person that created this Company was Gabriel de Usera, full professor at the University of Madrid.[17] This professor founded the Company, in 1961 with a joint venture with two well know Companies, Royal Insurance y Mercantile and General (both with 20% share).[18] But will have a dreadful development because the terrible earthquake in Managua in 1972 was too costly for the Company that had reinsure large quantities and disappeared completely in 1988 (Tortella et al. 2014, p. 352). The brother of Gabriel de Usera, Luis, was General Director since 1947 of one of the most important banks in Spain, the Hispano Americano and president of this bank since 1968 up to 1983. Financially had control of the insurance company La Estrella and Goya, Hispano-Inglesa de Reaseguros, S.A. was a captive company of La Estrella.[19]

Reaseguradora Colon, S.A. was created on 22 November 1972 in Madrid, with a nominal capital of 25,000,000 pesetas. It started with benefits the first two year but with a terrible loss in 1975 of 4,102,292 pesetas.

---

15 Document BOE-A-1990-5146.

16 Documento BOE-A-1997-14342.

17 Inspector of Insurance in the Ministry of Finance.

18 Gabriel Tortella *et al.* (2014), *La Historia del Seguro en España*, Madrid, Fundación Mapfre, p. 254.

19 José Luis García Ruiz (2014), "La bancaseguros en la crisis de la gran banca madrileña: el caso Hispano-Estrella", XI International Congress of the Economic History of the AEHE, Madrid, pp. 8–13.

The President was Abelardo Algora Marco and the Chief Executive Officer was Franciso López Rodríguez. The company will have a short life. The crisis of 1973 hit hard the financial market in Spain and wrong risk assume made the company ended already in December 1984 in the CLEA and it was eliminated from the civil registration of companies on 12 November 1989.[20]

We follow with Albatros Reaseguros created in 1976 by the Camuñas family. They also manage three insurance companies: Albia, Alboran and Mercantil. The executive responsible for Albatros was José María de Quinto, who had been the director of Goya, Hispano-Inglesa de Reaseguros, S.A. The earthquake in Mexico City in 1985 was a too big loss and was declared bankrupt.

Another company with a short life is REUNISA. This company was an attempt to create a reinsurance company controlled by Spanish insurance companies. As Spain did not have a big reinsurance company like France (SCOR), Germany (Munich RE) or Switzerland (Swiss RE) did. Many directors and president of Spanish insurance companies considered it necessary to create one and if a good number of Spanish insurance companies decided to create a reinsurance companies with financial capability it will make the difference and it seem a great idea. Eventually it was created (July 1975). It was very successful because 45 Spanish insurance companies were going to give financial support to the new company. However, the problem already started since the beginning, the moment was not the best, and the oil crisis hit nasty to the Spanish economy so the Spanish insurance companies did not provide much capital, only 284 million pesetas (each company shareholder could invest 10 million pesetas). Another problem was the management of the new company; it was a system of rotating presidencies established every four years. This prevented a strong executive management and long-term vision that is crucial in reinsurance. Four years after its establishment, in 1979, it had only 300 million pesetas. Alvaro Muñoz, president of MUSINI, tried unsuccessfully to extend the capital to 1,500 million pesetas. That would have allowed greater financial capability to develop the business. The lack of support of the Spanish insurance companies made that the experiment lasted barely until 1997. In May of that year it was cancelled from the official registration and it was liquidated.[21]

Finally, an even briefer story is Ocaso Reaseguros that will start in 1989. This company was a captive company of one of the big insurance companies in Spain: Seguros Ocaso, which had a great success in death insurance, initiated by Ramón D'Ortega y Hervella in 1920. The project was stop practically immediately because it was not so successful.[22]

---

[20] Document BOE-A-1990-5146.

[21] BOE-A-1997-14341992.

[22] Gabriel Tortella *et al.* (2014), p. 371.

The two companies that did survive the 20th century and still are appreciated today are Nacional de Reaseguros and Mapfre Re. Today the veteran is the first after the Spanish Civil War, it started on 15 December 1939 in Madrid. Nominal capital 12,000,000 pesetas and the President was Santiago Fuentes Pila, the General Director will be a person of great relevance in the Spanish insurance world, José Mª Sunyer Basseda, born in Reus (Tarragona) in 1898. Doctor in Law at the University of Madrid. Had been the responsible of the group of Reinsurance in the Sindicato Vertical the trade union of Insurance. This was the fascist union in the time of Franco regime (1939–1975). The managers and the workers were together so few strikes in this time of the history of Spain. Both sons of Doctor Synyer will follow the business: José María Sunyer Aldoma, General Director also of this company and of GES a direct insurance company. Carlos Sunyer Aldoma will be the Chief Executive Officer of Nacional de Reaseguros. Ignacio Hernando de Larramendi (General Manager in Mapfre) consider that the son Carlos with José Antonio Aparicio and José Ruiz will make this Company extremely competitive and with high excellency that will make it possible to be in the top of the reinsurance companies all along this period.[23] Its business will operate mainly in Spain, Italy, France and Portugal. In 2012, 80% of Nacional de Reaseguros premiums were from the Spanish market, 7.5% from Italy, 2.2% from France, 5.3% from Portugal and 5% from the rest of the world.

MAPFRE Re premiums were more diversified, with only 12% in Spain, 36% in other European countries, 32% in Latin America and 20% in other markets. Its early launch was in 1976, with a reinsurance company called MAPFRE Reaseguro, but faced serious problems, namely little capital and with tax contingencies, so it was taken over by Corporación MAPFRE in 1983. Nonetheless, it did not grow substantially until the late 1980s, when it opened offices in Manila, Caracas, Milan, Buenos Aires, London, Lisbon, Athens, Lima and Sao Paulo (Table 2). In addition, a specific reinsurance company was created: MAPFRE XL in 1986, to develop the business of non-proportional, which is the origin of MAPFRE Re. A big move ahead was made in 1988, when the company acquired 88% of the capital of Caja Reaseguradora in Chile, a state-owned company that was privatized. The acquisition gave much prestige to the Company in all Latin America. In 1989 the firm took over CIAR, a Belgium company founded in the 1970s, that owned the German company Iduana, two French companies, Azur and Maaf, an American company, Shelter Mutual, an Italian company, Societa Cattolica and the Swiss Mutuelle Valldoise. In 1991, MAPFRE acquired Reaseguradora Hemisférica in Colombia. It was still small, but it started to grow fast in the 1990s and

23 Ignacio Hernando de Larramendi (2000), *Así se hizo MAPFRE*, Madrid, Acta, p. 716.

transferred the reinsurance business to the Company in 2001. Finally, in 2000 they opened a branch office in London.

In the United States, the Company acquired Chatham Re, based in New Jersey, in 1999. It was owned by Ecclesiastical, a British company, which had connections with the Anglican Church. However, the technical reserves made it more profitable for the Company to absorb it in 2007 and the whole business was transferred to MAPFRE Re. The Company will take off already at the beginning of the 21st century. It ranked twentieth among the 2015 Non-Life Reinsurance Groups.[24]

Table 2. MAPFRE in reinsurance, 1984–1999

Año	País	Entidad
1984	México	Branch office
1986	Filipinas	Branch office
1988	Chile	Acquisition *Caja Reaseguradora de Chile*
1988	Venezuela	Branch office
1988	Italia	Branch office
1988	Luxemburgo	Maplux Re, Luxemburgo
1989	Bélgica	Acquisition CIAR, Bélgica
1990	Argentina	Branch office
1991	United Kingdom	Branch office
1991	Colombia	Acquisition *Reaseguradora Hemisférica*
1991	Portugal	Branch office
1993	Greece	Branch office
1996	Peru	Branch office
1996	Brazil	Branch office
1997	Belgium	Branch office
1999	United States	Acquisition *Chatham Re*

Source: MAPFRE archives.

The first big test for the Company was the earthquake in Mexico in 1985. The cost was enormous for the reinsurance market, over $3,387.4 m, and €2.4 m for the Company. The positive thing that happen was that

24 AM Best data & research, 5 Sept. 2016.

they paid fast, so it was regarded as a reliable company. The same happened when other natural disasters hit America: the hurricane Andrew in 1992, Georges and Mitch in 1998, and earthquakes in Chile in 1995 and 1997. Despite the losses, the company sorted out problems thanks to José Manuel Martínez and Andrés Jiménez, who spread risk and accumulated capital for this type of risk. Another problem for the company was the fiscal treatment in Spain. The solution was to create a specific company in Luxemburg, Maplux Re, to sort out the problem that was not solved until 1998. Finally, a big success was the XL premiums (excess of loss) because they sign with the most important reinsurance companies.

As all the efficient reinsurance companies, the Company knows well the insurance companies that sign reinsurance with them. Maybe we can point out two reasons for its success: networking, and staff involvement. At first, the company was successful in Latin America, a very risky market that was sorted out with a lot of work and less competition. On the other side, the European market was too costly, and the Company did not have the economic capability or the know-how of other companies to operate there.

At the end of the century in Spain, of all those attempts to develop a reinsurance company, practically 20 attempts, only two had been successful. In 2000 MAPFRE Re and Nacional de Reaseguros had premiums that were worth €787 m, MAPFRE Re €606.3 m and Nacional de Reaseguros €180.7 m.

Foreign reinsurance companies in Spain

One important conclusion that must be point out, that even the great efforts to create Spanish reinsurance companies, they practically did not succeed in all the period. The presence of foreign reinsurance companies was relevant and mainly as we can see, because there were no big Spanish reinsurance companies. Even more, the government did not set up a state reinsurance company, as in other countries for example France with SCOR. Probably because insurance was not a major issue for the government, who focused on the development of a welfare state. In addition, Spanish reinsurance companies transferred a large amount of business to foreign reinsurance companies because it was technically necessary. The foreign companies provided capacity per risk and in some way clogged coinsurance or national reinsurance, thus obstructing the growth of a domestic market. From a Schumpeterian perspective, this was a vicious circle and we have the evidence that many reinsurance companies did start, but only two survive and managed to get out of the vicious circle. Spanish reinsurance companies faced several problems:

1) Unbalanced portfolios. The premium income did not cover the liabilities undertaken. The home market was very small: it did not produce enough premium and did not have enough spread. In addition, the major problem related to a small market is that companies are undercapitalized, that is, they do not "share capital nor their free assets match the exposures that they cover".[25]
2) Reinsurance needs a big investment and develops over the long term. Spanish reinsurance companies had not been operating for a long time.
3) Even if the technical result was fine, the profit was small, so it did not bring more capital.
4) National companies covered the least capital.
5) Reserves were low, because companies paid less tax and a lower dividend.

As a result, in general the national reinsurance companies did not increase their assets. With the internal documents of the Mutual name Musini, we have a fine example of the difficulties that normally the Spanish insurance companies had with Spanish reinsurance.

Musini was created in 1966 and will insure all the companies of the State Holding Company INI (Instituto Nacional de Industria) similar to the Italian IRI, they had many big companies in heavy industry for example electricity: Endesa, steel: like Ensidesa, or in refineries of petrol that in Spain was a State monopoly (with the exception of the Canary Islands). INI will have over 150 companies and over 800,000 workers in the late 1970s.

The Board of directors of Musini explained the dependency of international reinsurance that insisted on prevention and protection that enforces sophisticated techniques that in Spain was missing. There was little know how about managing risk or maybe is better said that the most advance about it was in more advance countries, for example Germany. They remember that protection should be introduced "because we must also keep in mind that insurance is not just us, but it is in the second step, in reinsurance, and international reinsurance in industrial risks increasingly demands better information and higher security measures". "The reason is clear: industrial technology has advanced greatly, the size of the plants, the danger of the processes. It is not something that affects only Musini, not only Spain, it is worldwide and thus the reinsurance, which ultimately assumed in the economic risk, and demands more guarantees".[26]

In the case of Musini the relevant reinsurance company will be Munich Re, this company will bring experts to analyse the risk assume in each com-

25 UN 1980, p. 30.

26 Board of directors: 21 June 1972.

pany of the INI. There was an interesting story about a very sophisticated truck that brought high technology to supervise all the risky. The board of directors of Musini were fascinated with this truck that eventually will be bought by Musini. In addition, they will develop full courses of how to manage risk with experts from Spain and also from several other countries.

As we can see it is more about know how than money, but obviously, that does count too. For example, in the case of the coinsurance of Iberia (company that was of the Holding of the INI in the 1970s). There was AGARA the Spanish reinsurance pool that only held 1.13% of the total; the rest went mainly on foreign reinsurance. The exact amount was only 829,337 pesetas reinsure by AGARA, the rest 98.87% mainly abroad! One of the members of the board Fernández of Musini said of this incredible figure that it "shows the little effort they are doing the Spanish reinsurance as such for the reinsurance of an important company like Iberia". In fact, the Spanish pool were only brokers that past all the business to companies such as Munchener, Bayerische and Frankona from Munich, or Gerline-Konzern y Kolnische in Cologne. In those days, it was a political gold of the government to reinsure with Spanish companies, but as for example, AGARA did not have the financial capacity to reinsure.

The development of insurance and reinsurance

Direct insurance in Spain has experienced big changes in the last 35 years. Premiums used to account for only 2% of GDP. Big industries, transport companies or wealthy people only signed the cost of underwriting a policy in the 1960s. Anyway, it will change thanks to motor insurance, which started to develop far more already in the late 1960s, health insurance far more in the 1980s and life insurance far more in the 1990s. Life insurance was considered only for rich people, so that it had a poor development, unlike other Western European countries, as indicated in Table 2.

Table 2. Life insurance 1982. Premiums/GDP

Spain	1
Italy	1.18
France	4.41
Germany	9.23
Sweden	10.05
Holland	10.18
UK	11.59

Source: OCDE.

If, in 1965, there were in the world 144 reinsurance companies and premiums amounted to €23.31 m, with eleven pure reassures that accounted for over 40% of all premiums. In Spain, they were few and small. Table 3 presents the top ten Spanish reinsurance companies at the time.

Table 3. Reinsurance companies' premiums in Spain

Ranking		€ million	(%)
1	Compañía Española de Reaseguros (CERSA)	3.47	14.87
2	Compañía Ibérica de Reaseguros	1.98	8.50
3	Nacional de Reaseguros	1.28	5.49
4	Reaseguradora Española (RESA)	0.72	3.11
5	Continental	0.51	2.18
6	Garantía	0.45	1.92
7	Hispano Inglesa de Reaseguros	0.43	1.86
8	Sociedad Anónima Española de Reaseguros Nacionales e Internacionales (SAERNI)	0.28	1.21
9	Equitativa Reaseguro	0.18	0.78
10	Guipúzcoa	0.14	0.61
	Total	9.44	40.52

Source: *Seguros* (1966).

The reinsurance business grew substantially between 1965 and 2000 (see Appendix, Table 1). It multiplied 54 times, reaching €1,259 m. Big insurance companies accepted reinsurance from other countries. Their profits in the international markets made them accept even more reinsurance premiums mainly with brokers and subscription agencies. The new subscribers, described as "innocent subscribers", made up pools of reassurance that brought big losses for the insurance companies. Consequently, the companies wound up in the 1990s that is why mostly pure reinsurers subsequently did almost all the subscriptions.

The figures for the reinsurance market at the beginning of the 1980s shows the great dependency of the Spanish market with the world reinsurance market. In the Spanish Statistics of Reinsurance indicates that in 1980 of the 267,400 million pesetas in premiums they were 80,300 million pesetas of outwards reinsurance (ceded in the international market). It does represent 30% that is similar in that year to the development in Germany. The problem in the Spanish market was that Spanish reinsurance business was only 21,600 million pesetas of inward reinsurance (foreign companies that ceded to Spanish reinsurance companies), that was more or less one fourth of the reinsurance that is manage in the international market (26.9%). Spain had probably one of the worst percentage between outwards reinsurance and inward reinsurance in the world. Italy was far better with 75%.

José Manuel Martínez was very critical with the Spanish market of reinsurance and he pointed out three main problems: (a) large percentage of outwards reinsurance, (b) negative technical result and (c) low technical qualification that naturally did not introduce new types of premiums, basically only proportional reinsurance, the others will develop in the market latter. This are: reinsurance stop loss, excess of loss reinsurance, facultative reinsurance, facultative proportional reinsurance, average loss reinsurance, and so on.

The first problems that José Martínez point out, was that the Spanish reinsurance companies did not develop sufficiently simple risk. This lack, forces the necessity for another reinsurer, normally foreign for example Swiss Re, Munich Re or SCOR, all or a great part the insurance risk written by a ceding company because the high percentage of major risk in the portfolio of the first reinsurance company.

Anyway, he adds, this problem was less terrible in one of the most important risk, major catastrophe, which has generated so many problems in the reinsurance market in the last two decades. In the Spain reinsurance market the public company name Consorcio de Compensación de Seguros was useful in covering the risk on major catastrophes. In this period, the 1980s or 1990s it was very doubtful that any private Spanish company could assume this type of risk.

Another problem was the small risk accepted by Spanish reinsurance companies (detainment). Historically was common in the Spanish reinsurance, maybe because the companies want to assure benefit, between reinsurance commissions and cost, instead of reinsure related to their volume of portfolio and assets. However, we must explain that many reinsurance companies or insurance companies that develop reinsurance because they did not have the financial capability (few assets), so they can only be intermediaries.

Negative technical results, at the beginning of the 1980s in 1980, 1981 and 1982 the losses were 12,161 million of pesetas, 1,892 million the next year and 21,939 million in 1982. They were many reasons for the losses, such as many claims, but in addition, it must be explained by the great competition and the high-risk assumption with low premiums. Finally, the lack of know-how that did not introduce the entire great variety of reinsurance capable to develop the modern companies specialized in reinsurance.

Even if in Spain the development started in the first 35 years of the 20th century in a positive way (Gutiérrez and Pons, 2015). Nevertheless, with the Spanish Civil War and the autarky period, the development was not so positive, they even reduce their number since 1950 to 1980, from 13 to 11 companies, especially in reinsurance or pure reinsurance companies. In addition, all were relatively small and the first four were related to groups of direct insurance. In those days, Spain was not an exception to de world market, because mainly they were few countries that develop the business.

Another important question in reinsurance is time. To build up a great company in reinsurance you need to be successful of course and normally a long period gaining the credibility and expertise that is achieve by learning by doing. Of the main companies in the world in 1980, four started in the 19th century: Cologne Re (1846), Swiss Re Group (1863), Munich Re (1880) and Frankona (1886). Another four at the beginning of the 20th century: Mercantile & General Reinsurance Group (1907), Employers Re Group (1914), American Re (1917), and General Re Group (1921) and only two of the second half of the 20th century: Gerling Group (1954) and Prudential Re Group (1973). Both started with the important support of major companies in direct insurance.

This was a thought of José Manuel Martínez that started MAPFRE Re with the perfect understanding that it need time to achieve success.

In Spain reinsurance companies developed very little reinsurance with other countries. There were some unsuccessful attempts. La Unión y El Fénix Español and other companies made an attempt with a reinsurance company called CERSA. La Estrella with another reinsurance company, Goya. As we already said, of the 11 reinsurance companies in 1965, only one survived, Nacional de Reaseguros, which started in 1939 and operated mainly in Spain, Italy, France and Portugal.

Conclusion

Reinsurance is essential for the insurance market; in fact, the insurance market would not exist without the large reinsurance market. This market has significantly changed during the second half of the 20th century; the reason of its importance is the four main solutions that solves in the insurance market: financing, stabilization, capacity, and catastrophe protection. Few companies dominate this market. Europe is the main continent to develop reinsurance, and the United States is far behind. It is better to refer to companies and not countries, because in fact they are few companies that control the reinsurance market and is a minor issue for the economies of the countries. Finally, we can add that there is no big reinsurance company in the major center for reinsurance. London maybe proves how confusing the market is.

In the chapter, we explain how is outstanding that a developing country like Spain ends up as a develop country in the European Union. Spain is successful in its caching up process. However, it has been a very long process for the Spanish pure reinsurance companies. Mainly because the characteristics of the country was of developing countries. In side Spain, they will have a great dominance of the market the foreign companies such as Munich Re or Swiss Re or few others; anyway, they will help the catching up process in Spain. They will bring know how and financial capability.

This development will be done even if they were many restrictions to the foreign companies and capital. The government of Franco had the strong belief that the Spanish companies can do it better than the foreign companies can. As we explain, if before the Spanish Civil War there was two companies, after they will be created 19 more. There is a great moment of willing to create Spanish reinsurance companies, especially in the 1940s. The managers of these companies had great belief in their capability, but in addition, they expected a Spanish law that defend above all this numerous development of Spanish companies.

In the 1960s and 1970s the national insurance companies tried to develop Spanish reinsurance, but the lack of sufficient capital, made it very difficult, several attempts were developed, but mainly were failures with only two exceptions of small capacity: Nacional de Reaseguros and the beginning of MAPFRE Re.

This situation changed in the 1980s and 1990s, when MAPFRE Re develop business in the international market. This, together with successful management is the reasons for its success. MAPFRE Re stands out as the 20th biggest Non-Life Reinsurance Groups of the world in 2015. Finally, in the case of Nacional de Reaseguros, very efficient but mainly develops all its business in Spain and remains as a small company.

Appendix

Table 1. Reinsurance premiums in peseta (not life)

1946	359,517,375
1947	546,981,605
1948	585,712,417
1949	752,216,827
1950	954,784,229
1951	1,122,474,597
1952	1,111,553,325
1953	1,224,817,953
1954	1,279,700,000
1955	1,349,058,257
1956	1,557,839,704
1957	1,565,926,102
1958	1,613,451,959
1959	2,108,459,743
1960	2,275,958,551
1961	2,452,700,000
1962	2,735,800,000
1963	3,388,000,000
1964	3,974,300,000
1965	4,101,798,768
1966	5,654,163,993
1967	6,082,837,784
1968	6,300,000,000
1969	nd
1970	6,664,396,000
1971	6,738,820,000
1972	7,337,360,000
1973	7,835,810,000

1974	8,948,200,000
1975	10,121,230,000
1976	12,515,310,000
1977	14,800,850,000
1978	17,880,750,000
1979	18,420,870,000
1980	21,593,100,000
1981	24,232,560,000
1982	28,661,380,000
1983	28,524,320,000
1984	31,713,760,000
1985	34,081,100,000
1986	40,094,900,000
1987	55,065,400,000
1994	72,872,000,000
2000	209,480,000,000 (1)

Sources: *Anuario Español de Seguros.* (1) all reinsurance premiums.

Table 2. Premiums paid for reinsurance accepted in Spain in the different branches during 1949

Companies	**Premiums**
Compañía Mediterránea de Reaseguros	105,136,985
Compañía Española de Reaseguros (C.E.R.)	65,154,007
Compañía General de Reaseguros[1]	51,400,227
La Equitativa Hispano Americana	50,497,972
La Equitativa (P. R.) Reaseguros	43,000,493
La Unión y El Fénix Español	38,728,583
Reaseguradora Española, S.A.	27,841,971

1 Resolución de la Dirección General de Banca, Bolsa e Inversiones por la que se hace público la eliminación de la Compañía General de Reaseguros, S.A. del Registro de Compañías. *Boletín Oficial del Estado* No. 182, de 31/07/1959, página 10392. Orden de 8 de enero de 1959 por la que se dispone la disolución de la "Compañía General de Reaseguros, Sociedad Anónima" domiciliada en Barcelona. *Boletín Oficial del Estado* No. 55, de 05/03/1959, página 3715.

Companies	Premiums
Assicurazioni Generali	25,257,525
Nacional de Reaseguros, S.A.	22,173,093
Continetal Compañía Española de Reaseguros	19,966,016
Compañía Hispano Americano de Seguros Generales	19,252,642
Plus Ultra. Compañía Anónima de Seguros Generales	16,976,625
Minerva, S.A.	16,335,576
Covadonga, S.A. de Seguros	14,690,861
Cervantes, S.A.	12,299,113
C.I.A., Comercio, Industria y Agricultura	10,453,937
La Estrella, S.A.	9,244,483
Banco Vitalicio de España	7,082,747
La Vasco Navarra, S.A. de Seguros y Reaseguros	6,983,657
Mare Nostrum, S.A. de Seguros y Reaseguros	6,647,532
Compañía Adriática de Seguros	6,647,532
La Victoria de Berlín, S.A.	6,275,938
El Porvenir de los Hijos	5,865,404
Consorcio Español de Reaseguradores	5,389,104
La Previsión Española	4,926,561
Garantía, S.A. de Reaseguros	4,801,830
Andalucía, Compañía de Seguros Generales	4,516,520
La Paternal	4,422,435
Madrid, S.A. de Seguros Generales	4,342,662
La Economía	4,244,862
General Española de Seguros, S.A.	4,175,925
Aurora, Compañía Anónima de Seguros	4,166,414
Campo, Compañía de Seguros Agrícolas	4,165,753
Orión, Compañía Española de Seguros	4,159,618
Occidente	4,125,897
La Polar	3,972,355
Omnia, S.A.E. Compañía de Seguros	3,777,968
Unión Española, Compañía de Seguros	3,472,775
Guipúzcoa, S.A., Reaseguros	3,351,192
El Fénix Español Agrícola	3,338,660

Companies	Premiums
Atlántida, Compañía Hispano Americano de Seguros	3,336,254
La Sud América	3,322,671
Nacional Hispánica Aseguradora	3,050,932
La Constancia. Compañía Anónima de Seguros	3,037,832
Unión Levantina, S.A. de Seguros	2,779,703
Lucero, Sociedad Anónima de Seguros	2,756,478
La Patria Hispana, S.A. de Seguros	2,706,083
Cresa, Compañía de Seguros y Reaseguros	2,521,724
Centro de Navieros Aseguradores	2,486,025
Multimar	2,334,683
El Hércules Hispano	2,159,248
La Mundial, Sociedad Anónima	2,085,541
Unión Iberoamericana	2,082,597
Compañía Internacional de Seguros	2,080,172
Unión Pacífico, S.A.	2,048,002
Aragón, Compañía Anónima de Seguros	2,033,017
Hermes, Compañía Anónima de Seguros	2,003,480
Nervión, Reaseguros, S.A.	1,940,607
Vizcaya, S.A. de Seguros y Reaseguros	1,894,813
La Suiza, Compañía Anónima de Seguros Generales	1,830,716
La Equitativa Nacional	1,814,539
Centro Levantino de Seguros y Reaseguros	1,701,227
S.I.C.A. Seguros Industriales	1,576,795
Fides, Compañía Española de Seguros	1,476,420
La Previsión Nacional	1,371,809
Península r, S.A. de Seguros	1,289,522
Bilbao, Compañía Anónima de Seguros	1,245,374
Universo, S.A. de Seguros	1,193,739
Fomento Español de Seguros	1,171,026
Mutuelle Générale Francaise-Vie	1,138,817
Meridional, Compañía Anónima de Seguros	1,133,978
Le Phénix, S.A. de Seguros-Vida	1,097,425
L'Union, Incendios, Accidentes y Riesgos Diversos	1,089,524

Companies	**Premiums**
L'Union-Vida	1,039,626
La Previsora Hispalense, S.A.	1,029,585
Institución Aseguradora (I.A.S.A.)	874,305
Cantabria	852,581
Levante, Sociedad Italiana de Seguros y Reaseguros	843,276
Galicia, S.A. de Seguros y Reaseguros	793,144
El Aguila, Compañía de Seguros contra Incendios	779,183
Ibérica, S.A.	729,512
España, Compañía de Seguros	682,101
Nordstern, Compañía Anónima de Seguros	661,698
Sur, Compañía Española de Seguros	658,165
Nacional Suiza, Compañía de Seguros	656,143
Metrópolis, S.A.	642,501
Compañía Aragonesa de Seguros	606,560
Italia, Seguros	602,882
Aggippina	588,171
Vesta, Compañía Anónima de Seguros y Reaseguros	587,446
Royal Insurance Company Limited	584,743
Layetana, S.A. Compañia Española de Seguros	573,553
El Sol, Compañía de Seguros contra Incendios	534,205
Financiera Nacional	524,501
La Nationale-Incendios, Compañías de Seguros	523,601
Lepanto, S.A.	494,939
Lloyd Alemán, Compañía Anónima de Seguros	479,634
Velázquez, S.A.	475,624
El Sol, Compañía de Seguros contra Accidentes-Robo	472,506
Phoenix Assurance Company Limited	470,360
L'Abeille-Incendios	460,858
Du Phénix, Compañía Francesa de Seguros contra Incendios	451,150
The London & Lancashire Insurance	445,710
Consolidada, S.A. Hispao Americana	414,630
Commercial Union Assurance	396,489
C.A.S.E.R.	392,012

Companies	Premiums
La Unión Alcoyana	370,963
Wurtemburguesa y Badense	365,065
Caledonian Insurance Company	323,302
Alliance Assurance Company	314,157
Northern Assurance	291,382
Cúspide	288,970
Reliance Marine Insurance Company	276,955
Sun Insurance Office	257,879
Royal Exchange Assurance	239,089
Hispania, Compañía General de Seguros	215,905
Sociedad Catalana de Seguros	194,729
Pearl Assurance Company Limited	181,912
The Liverpool & London	179,838
Compagnie d'Assurance Générales-Incendios	169,670
O'Trabalho	161,104
The British & Foreign Marine	157,811
Guardian Assurance	155,277
Nord Deutsche, Compañía de Seguros	139,268
Legal & General Assurance	136,349
The World Marine & General Insurance	118,920
The Continental Assurance	113,260
The London Assurance	105,627
Mannheim	74,710
Le Assicurazioni d'Italia	61,662
La Urbana, Compañía de Seguros contra Incendios	55,717
El Norte, Compañía Anónima de Seguros	55,469
Iberia, Compañía Anónima de Seguros Generales	49,168
Compagnie d'Assurances Générales, Riesgos Diversos	45,479
L'Urbane-Vie	44,614
Báltica, Compañía Danesa de Seguros	35,247
La Federal, Compañía Anónima de Seguros	30,243
Mediodía, Compañía de Seguros y Reaseguros	28,681
Salvafilms, S.A.	24,021

Companies	**Premiums**
Aseguradora del Film, S.A.	21,208
North British and Mercantile Insurance	18,252
The Union Marine and General Insurance	16,157
Vital de Seguros	10,843
Instituto Nacionale delle Assicuracione	9,253
Caja de Previsión y Socorro	9,125
L'Abeille Pedrisco	4,536
Unión Ganadera	4,390
L'Abeille-Accidentes	4,003
The total of companies is 149.	

Graphic of the changes between 1949 and 1959 in premiums in reinsurance

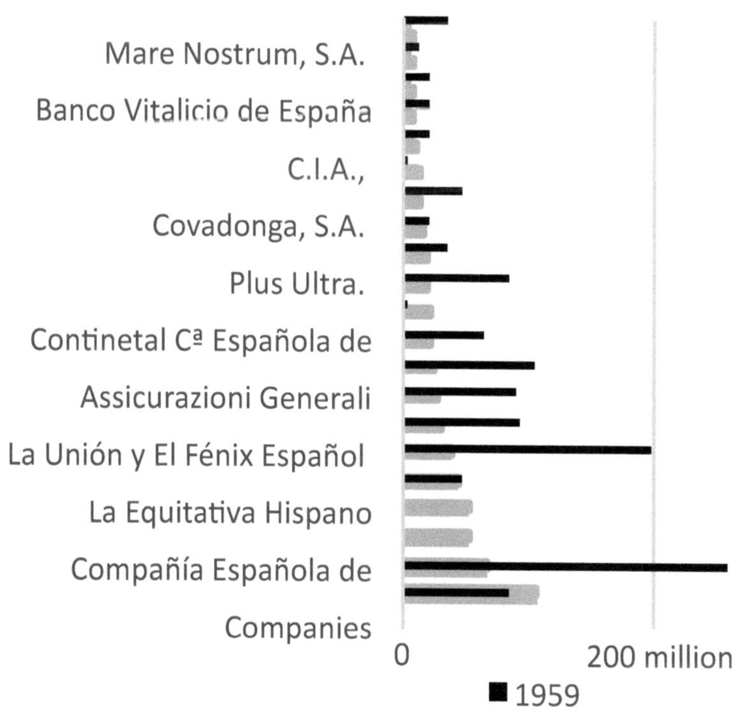

Temporary Concluding Remarks

Developments in reinsurance are not known to the public. Nevertheless, they are very well-known to insurance companies. This is because reinsurance companies assure the insurance companies. This book, *Highlights of Reinsurance History*, represents the final publication of the papers presented at the 17th World Congress of Economic History in Kyoto (2015). In this pleasant Japanese city, we saw the first results of an ongoing project. It will continue with other academic meetings as new steps in the research.

Reinsurance is one of the main actors in the insurance world. First, it allows the expansion of the insurance companies, and secondly, it plays a specific role in the case of big risk. After the 18th century, in order to assume more risk, the insurance market began with coinsurance. But this was not sufficient, and a more sophisticated system was developed from the mid-XIX century: reinsurance. Reinsurance companies grew and expanded throughout the world, even though they originated from only a handful of countries, Germany, Switzerland and France being the major players in the beginning. In fact, a very small number of companies, with huge capital, have control of the reinsurance market.

Why are these companies so important? Mainly because one of the main purposes of reinsurance is to manage the worst periods of the insurance industry better. We are referring here to earthquakes, hurricanes or any other major disaster, in the event of which, obviously, an insurance company cannot assume the risk alone. Of course, there is competition between the insurance companies, but in these hard-hitting circumstances they cannot survive alone: they need practically all the companies to assume the big risk, and this is why reinsurance has grown so fast in the insurance industry and has become so gigantic. The other option, coinsurance, basically did not grow, because the companies did not want the other companies to know about their business (with one huge exception, the Lloyd's market of London). Obviously, with coinsurance you had to explain in detail what you were assuring. In addition, the development of reinsurance presents several difficulties, sometimes positive ones and sometimes less so. For example, the relationship between insurers and reinsurers has involved battles over premium rates. Insurers normally need these to be low so as to be more competitive, whereas reinsurers increase them so as to guarantee the sustainability of the insurance companies. Another question is reciprocity, and the fact that reinsurance permits large amounts in deposit in insurers' accounts in order to allow them to expand their business.

At the end of the day, the reinsurance companies may decide prices, types of premiums, and what can be assured by the insurance companies and what cannot when the risk is new. Why this is so? Because in many cases, they have the know-how. They can calculate exactly what they can and cannot pay if there is a major disaster. This is also normally the case with big insurers: they work as a team.

How is this possible? The network is large and dense; not only do reinsurance companies develop reinsurance, but also insurance companies are reinsured and have captive reinsurance companies, and reinsurance companies have to be reinsured themselves. Finally, we cannot forget that today there is a strong tendency to use new tools in the financial markets that are considered reinsurers.

Another major player in reinsurance is the United States, as we have seen in the various chapters of this book. This was the case following the First World War and up till and after the Second World War, including in the new countries.

As was mentioned above, this is research that will continue. Our aim here has been to present in detail as many aspects as possible of this little-known industry.

Bibliography

Adams, Mike, Andersson, Lars Fredrik, Jia, Joy Yihui, Lindmark, Magnus, "Mutuality as a control for information asymmetry: a historical analysis of the claims experience of mutual and stock fire insurance companies in Sweden 1889-1939", *Business History*, 53 (2011), 1074-91.

Adiel, Ron, "Reinsurance and the Management of Regulatory Ratios and Taxes in the Property-Casualty Insurance Industry", *Journal of Accounting and Economics*, 22, (1996), 207-240.

Annan'ich Boris V., *Rossiia i mezhdunarodnyi Kapital, 1897-1914* (Russia and International Capital) (Leningrad, 1970).

Annan'ich Boris V., *Vlastì reform at samoderzhavnoi k sovetskoi Rossii* (Authority and reforms. Form autocratic to Soviet Russia) (St Petersburg 1996).

Annan'ich, Boris Vasilievich, Ganelin, Rafail Sholomovich, *SY Witte and his time* (St Petersburg: Dmitrii Bulanin, 1999).

Annan'ich B.V., "Denezhnaya reforma 1895-1897 i vvedenie zolotogo standarta". Istoriya Banka Rossii. 1860-2010 (Moscow, T. 1. S. 2010), 272-286.

Argus International (L'), *L'Argus International*, January 20, (1978).

Association of Life Insurance Companies in Japan, *The Meiji Taisho Hoken Shiryo* (Insurance Documents in the period of Meiji and Taisho), 4 Vols., 9 Books, 1934-1943 (Japanese).

Bähr, Johannes and Kopper, Christopher, *Munich Re. The Company History 1880-1980* (Munich: C.H. Beck, 2016).

Bergholm, Paul, *Återförsäkringsaktiebolaget Sverige 1914 11/11 1924. Några anteckningar rörande bolagets tillkomst och utveckling* [Sweden Re 1914 11/11 1924. A couple of notes concerning the creation and development] (Stockholm: Återförsäkringsaktiebolaget Sverige, 1925).

Best special report, *Global Reinsurance*, Segment Review. September 8, (2014).

Borscheid, Peter and Haueter, Niels Viggo (eds.), *World Insurance. The Evolution of a Global Risk Network* (Oxford: Oxford University Press, 2012).

Borscheid, Peter *et al.*, *Swiss Re und die Welt der Risikomärkte* (Munich: C.H. Beck, 2014).

Canals i Vilaró, Salvador, *Cuestiones económicas: el Comité Oficial de Seguros y el reaseguro obligatorio del Estado* (Barcelona: Revista Occidente, 1923).

Caruana de la Cagigas, Leonardo and García, José Luis, "La internacionalización del seguro español: el caso de Mapfre, 1969-200", *Informe Comercial Española*, ICE, No. 849. Julio-agosto (2009).

Dai Tokyo Fire and Marine Insurance Co. Ltd., *The History of Dai Tokyo Fire and Marine Insurance Company* (Japanese), Dai Tokyo Fire and Marine Insurance Co (2004).

Dai Tokyo Fire and Marine Insurance Co. Ltd., *The 50 Years History: Dai Tokyo Fire and Marine Insurance Company*, Dai Tokyo Fire and Marine Insurance Co (Japanese) (1971).

Deelstra, Griselda and Plantin, Eugene, *Risk theory and reinsurance* (London: Springer, 2014).

De Vogüe, P., "Professional Reinsurance and the problem of developing countries", *First Third World Insurance Congress in Manila* (1977).

Dickson P.G.M., *The Sun Insurance Office 1710-1960. The history of two and a half centuries of British Insurance* (Oxford: Oxford University Press, 1960).

Doherty, Neil & Kent Smetters, "Moral hazard in reinsurance markets", *Journal of Risk and Insurance*, 72/3 (2005), 375-391.

Dowa Fire and Marine Insurance Company, Ltd., *The 50 Years History of Dowa Fire, a Complete History* (Japanese), Dowa Fire and Marine Insurance Company (1995).

Efimov S.L., Akimov V.V., Borzyh V.N., *Strahovoe delo v Rossii: vehi istorii* (Moscow, Russkoe slovo, 1997).

Englund, Karl, *Återförsäkringsaktiebolaget Sverige 1914-1939. Redogörelse för bolagets verksamhet under de tjugofem första åren* [Sweden Re 1914-1939. An account for the corporation's during the first 25 years] (Stockholm: Ivar Haeggströms, 1940).

Englund, Karl, "Märkesmän inom svenskt försäkringsväsen. Biografiska snabbteckningar" [Prominent men within Swedish insurance industry], *Gjallarhornet* (1945).

Englund, Karl, *Insurance companies on the move: From Skandia to the Skandia group, 1855-1980* [Stockholm: Skandia, 1982].

Englund, Karl, *Skandiamän och andra försäkringsmän 1855-1970. Femtio biografiska studier* [Men from Skandia and other insurance men 1855-1970. Fifty biographical studies] (Stockholm: Skandia, 1993).

Feygin Y.A., "Perestrakhovanie, ego istoriya i sovremennoe polozhenie", (Reinsurance, its history and the contemporary situation), *Strakhovoe obozrenie*. 10. (An overview of insurance) 1915.

Fourastié, Jean, *Les Assurances au point de vue économique et social* (Paris: Payot, 1946).

Frax Rosales, Esperanza y Matilla Quiza, María Jesús, 'Los seguros en España: 1830-1934', *Revista de Historia Económica* 14/1 (1996), 183-203.

Fuji Fire and Marine Insurance Co. Ltd., *Fuji Fire: 70 Years History* (Japanese) (1989).

García Ruiz, José Luis, "La bancaseguros en la crisis de la gran banca madrileña: el caso Hispano-Estrella", *XI International Congress of Economic History of the AEHE*, Madrid (2014).

García Ruiz, José Luis and Caruana de la Cagigas, Leonardo, "La internacionalización del seguro español en el siglo XX", *Revista de Historia Industrial*, 41/3 (2009), 17-48.

Garethewohl, Klaus, *Reinsurance. Principles and Practice*. 1-2 (Karlsruhe: Versicherungswirtschaft, 1980 and 1982).

Gerathewohl, Klaus, *Reaseguro. Teoría y Práctica* (Madrid: Reaseguros Gil y Carvajal, 1993).

Global Reinsurance Highlights (New York: Standard & Poor's Ratings Services, a part of McGraw Hill Financial Inc. several years).

Global reinsurance capital, split traditional and alternative – Source: Aon Benfield, several years.

Gobert, Joseph, *Etude sur la réassurance, ses avantages, ses dangers et son importance économique* (Bruxelles: A. de Reume, 1923).

Golding, Cecil Edward, *A history of reinsurance, with sidelights on insurance*. Offered as a memento of fifty years' service in the reinsurance world by Sterling offices limites (London: Sterling, 1927).

Gregory, Paul, *Russian National Income, 1885-1913* (Cambridge: Cambridge University Press, 1982).

Grenholm, Åke and Harald Cramér, *Filip Lundberg. Förgrundsman i svensk livförsäkring* [Filip Lundberg. Pioneer within Swedish life insurance] (Stockholm: Svenska Livförsäkringsbolags Förening, 1969).

Gutiérrez, Pablo, *El control de divisas durante el primer franquismo. La intervención del reaseguro (1940-1952)* (Madrid: Banco de España, 2014).

Gutiérrez, Pablo and Pons, Jerònia, "Risk management and reinsurance strategies in the Spanish insurance market (1880-1940)", *Business History*, (2016).

Gürtler, Max, *Betriebswirtschaftliche Probleme des Versicherungswesens* (Wiesbaden: Dr. Th. Gabler, 1959).

Hagopian, Mikaël, *Dix leçons dur la réassurance* (Paris: l'Argus 1981).

Hagopian, Mikaël, Laparra, Michel et Bigot, Jean (prêt), *Aspects théoriques et pratiques de la réassurance* (Paris: l'Argus, 1991).

Hernando de Larramendi, Ignacio, *Así se hizo MAPFRE* (Madrid: Acta, 2000).

Herzog, Martin, *Was Dokumente erzählen können – Zur Geschichte der Münchener Rück* (Munich: unpublished typoscript, 1974-1992) (Munich Re Corporate Archive).

Hirao, H. (Anzai, T. revised), *Hirao Hachisabuto Jiden* (The Autobiography of Hirao Hachisaburo), Nagoya (Japanese) (1996).

http://dx.doi.org/10.1080/00076791.2016.1187136.

http://www.constitution.org/bouv/bouvierr.txt.

International Insurance Monitor, April (1979).

Ikema, M., Inoue, Y., Nishizawa, T., and Yamauchi, S. (eds.), *Hitotsubashi University 1975-2000, A Hundred and Twenty-five Years of Higher Education in Japan* (London: MacMillan, 2000).

James, Harold, Borscheid, Peter, Gugerli, David, Straumann, Tobias, *The value of risk. Swiss Re and the history of reinsurance* (Oxford: Oxford University Press, 2013).

Jannott, Horst, "Einige aktuelle Kernfragen der Assekuranz aus der Sicht eines Rückversicherers", *Versicherungswirtschaft* 34 (1979), 283-286.

Japan Business History Institute (ed.), *The 125 Years History of Tokio Marine* (Japanese), (2005).

Japan Business History Institute (ed.), *The 75 Years History of Mitsui Marine and Fire Insurance* (Japanese), (1996).

Japan Business History Institute (ed.), *The Centenary History of Sumitomo Marine and Fire Insurance* (Japanese), (1995).

Japan Business History Institute (ed.), *The Centenary History of Tokio Marine and Fire Insurance, Ltd., Vol. 1 and Vol. 2* (Japanese), (1979, 1982).

Johnson, Richard E., "Reinsurance: Theory, the New Applications, and the Future", *The Journal of Risk and Insurance*, 44/1 (1977).

Kamiya, H., "The background on the formation of the Union for Hull Insurers, Japanese marine insurance business in the 1920s", *Songai-hoken Kenkyu* (Review of General Insurance) 74 (3) (Japanese), (2012).

Kamiya, H., "The emergence of competition in the Japanese marine insurance business and the premium cartel", *Keiei Shigaku* (Japanese Business History Review), 44 (4) (Japanese), (2010).

Kon, G. and Kitazawa, Y. (eds.), *Nihon ni okeru Kasai-hoken Ryoritsu Kyotei Enkakushi* (The History of Tariff Agreement for Fire Insurance in Japan), 1 & 2 (Japanese), (1944).

Kopf, FCAS, Edwin W., "The Origin and Development of Reinsurance", *Proceedings of the Casualty* Actuarial Society, XVI (1929).

Korelin, Avenir P., Stepanov, S., *Yu. Witte – finisist, politik, diplomat* (Moscow, Terra, 1998).

La Réassurance (Paris, mensuel, 1917-1977).

Larsson, Mats and Mikael Lönnborg, and Sven-Erik Svärd, *Den svenska försäkringsmodellens uppgång och fall* [The rise and fall of the Swedish insurance model] (Stockholm: Svenska Försäkringsföreningens Förlag, 2005).

Larsson, Mats and Mikael Lönnborg, "Ömsesidig försäkringsverksamhet och den svenska försäkringsmodellen [Mutual Insurance and the Swedish Insurance Model]", *Scandinavian Insurance Quarterly*/1, (2007), 85-100.

Larsson, Mats and Mikael Lönnborg, "Den svenska finansmarknaden i ett långsiktigt perspektiv [The Swedish financial market from a long term perspective]", in Gunvall Grip (ed.), *Folksam 1908-2008. Mer än endast försäkring* [Folksam 1908-2008. More Than Only Insurance], 2 (Stockholm: Informationsförlaget, 2009a), 210-255.

Larsson, Mats and Mats Lönnborg, "Samverkan och konkurrens inom svensk försäkring [Collaboration and competition within the Swedish insurance market]", in Gunvall Grip (ed.), *Folksam 1908-2008. Mer än endast försäkring*

[Folksam 1908-2008. More Than Only Insurance], 2 (Stockholm: Informationsförlaget, 2009b), 179-209.

Larsson, Mats and Lönnborg, M., "The History of Insurance Companies in Sweden: 1855-2005", in Caruana de las Cagigas, L. (ed.), *Encuentro Internacional sobre la Historia del Seguro* (Madrid: Fundació Mapfre, 2010), 197-237.

Larsson, Mats and Mikael Lönnborg, *SCOR Sweden Re. 100 Years of Swedish (Re).* Insurance History (Stockholm: Dialogos, 2014a).

Larsson, Mats and Mikael Lönnborg, *Finanskriser i Sverige* [Financial Crises in Sweden] (Lund: Studentlitteratur, 2014b).

Larsson, Mats and Mikael Lönnborg, "The Survival and Success of Swedish Mutual Insurers", in Robin Pearson, and Takau Yoneyama (eds.), *Corporate Forms and Organisational Choice in International Insurance* (Oxford: Oxford University Press, 2015), 93-113.

Larsson, Mats and Mikael Lönnborg, "Regulation competition of Swedish Insurance Business. The Role of the insurance cartel registry", in Susanna Fellman, and Martin Shanahan (eds.), *Regulating Competition: Cartel Registers in the Twentieth Century World* (Abingdon & New York: Routledge: 2016), 248-267.

Larsson, Tage, "The men, ideas and activities", in *Sweden Reinsurance Company 1914-1964* (Stockholm: Återförsäkringsaktiebolaget Sverige, 1965).

Leblanc, Henri, *La réassurance du point de vue économique* (Paris: L.G.D.J., 1949).

Liljegren, Josef and Andersson, Lars-Fredrik, "Variation in organizational form across lines of property insurance: Sweden, 1913-1939", *Financial History Review*, 21 (2014), 77-101.

Lönnborg, Mikael, "Internationalisering av svenska försäkringsbolag. Drivkrafter, organisering och utveckling 1855-1913" [Internationalization of Swedish Insurers. Driving forces, organization and development 1855-1914]. *Uppsala Studies in Economic History* 46 (Uppsala: Acta Universitatis Upsaliensis, 1999).

Lundberg, Filip and Harry Molén, *Utvecklingslinjer inom svensk livförsäkring. Minnesskrift med anledning av Svenska livförsäkringsbolags förenings 50-års jubileum* [The development of the Swedish life insurance industry. Anniversary to celebrate the 50 year of Swedish Life Insurance Association] (Stockholm: Svenska Livförsäkringsbolags Förening, 1958).

Manes, Alfred, *Versicherungswesen* (Leipzig: B.G. Teubner, 1913).

Materialy po istorii SSSR.

Mayers, David and Smith, Clifford, "On the corporate demand for insurance", *Journal of Business*, 55 (1982), 281-96.

Mayers, David and Smith, Clifford, "On the corporate demand for insurance: evidence from the reinsurance market", *Journal of Business*, 63 (1990), 19-40.

Materialy po istorii SSSR.

Mitsui Marine & Fire Insurance Co. Ltd., *Building Protection, The Story of Mitsui Marine & Fire Insurance 1918-1993*, Tokyo, Mitsui Marine & Fire Insurance Co. Ltd, (1994).

Modigliani, Franco and Millar, Merton, "The cost of capital, corporation finance and the theory of investment", *The American economic Review*, 48 (1958), 261-297.

Münchener Rückversicherungs-Gesellschaft, Geo Risks Research, NatCatSERVICE (2010).

Munich Re Corporate Archive (HAMR).

Munich Reinsurance Company, *Reinsurance, What It Can Do For You* (1963).

Nichido Fire and Marine Insurance Co. Ltd. (1954). *The 40 Years History of Nichido Fire and Marine Insurance Company* (Japanese).

Palme, Sven, *Thule under 50 år* [Thule during 50 years] (Stockholm: Hæggström, 1923).

Pearson, Robin, "The development of reinsurance markets in Europe during the nineteenth century", *Journal of European Economic History*, 24 (1995), 557-72.

Pearson, Robin, "The birth pains of a global reinsurer. Swiss Re of Zürich, 1864-79", *Financial History Review*, 8 (2001), 27-47.

Pearson, Robin, *Insuring the Industrial Revolution: fire insurance in Great Britain, 1700-1850* (London: Ashgate, 2004).

Pearson, Robin, "Las compañías de seguros en España antes de 1914", in Jerònia Pons Pons and María Ángeles Pons Brías (eds.), *Investigaciones históricas sobre el seguro español* (Madrid: Fundación MAPFRE, 2010), 101-30.

Pearson Robin (ed.), *The Development of International Insurance* (London: Pickering and Chatto, 2010).

Pearson, Robin, and Yoneyama, Takau (eds.), *Corporate Forms and Organizational Choice in International Insurance* (Oxford: Oxford University Press, 2015).

Petrov Yuri, A., "Ekonomicheskoe polozhenie imperii v nachale XX", in A.N. Yakolev (ed.), *Rossiya v nachale XX veka* (The economic situation of the empire at the start of the 20th centuary) (Moscow: Noviy khronograf, 2002).

Petrov, Yuri, "Russia: Early expansion, state involvement, and re-emergence of the insurance industry", in Peter Borscheid and Niels V. Haueter (eds.), *World Insurance. The Evolution of a Global Risk Network* (Oxford: Oxford University Press, 2012), 213-238.

Petrov, Yury A. and Tatarinov, S.V. *Istoriya Banka Rossii. 1860-2010*: v 2 (Moscow, 2010).

Picard, Marice et Besson, André, "les assurances terrestres en Droit français", *Revue internationale de droit comparé*, 23, 1 (1971) 270-271.

Pons, Jerònia, *Las estrategias de crecimiento de las compañías de seguros en España, 1900-1940* (Madrid: FUNEP, 2002).

Pons, Jerònia, "Diversificación y cartelización en el seguro español, 1914-1935", *Revista de Historia Económica*, 21 (2003), 567-592.

Pons, Jerònia, "The influence of foreign companies in the organization of the Spanish insurance market: diversification and cartelisation 1880-1939", in Peter Borscheid and Robin Pearson (eds.), *Internationalisation and globalisa-*

tion of the insurance industry in the 19th and 20th centuries (Zurich: Marburg University, 2007), 49-65.

Pons, Jerònia, "Multinational enterprises and institutional regulation in the life insurance market in Spain 1880-1935", *Business History Review*, 82 (2008), 87-114.

Pons Pons, Jerònia, "A History of insurance companies in Spain until 1936", in Instituto de Ciencias del Seguro, *Encuentro internacional sobre la Historia del seguro* (Madrid: Fundación MAPFRE, 2010), 141-74.

Pons, Jerònia and Gutiérrez, Pablo, "The actuarial practices of British life insurance companies in peripheral countries: the case of Spain (1890-1936)", *Enterprise and Society*, 17/2 (2016), 237-264.

Pons Pons, Jerònia, *130 años de promesas cumplidas. Grupo Zurich en España*, Editorial Planeta, Barcelona (2016).

Powell, Lawrence and Somner, David, "Internal versus external capital markets in the insurance industry: The role of insurance", *Journal of Financial Services Research*, 31 (2007), 173-88.

Prieto, Eugenio, *El reaseguro: función económica* (Madrid: ICE, 1973).

Pruitt, Dudley M., "The Seat of Wisdom", *Proceedings of the Castualty Actuarial Society*, XLV, (1958).

Raynes, H. E., *A history of British insurance* (London: Pitman, 1950).

Richard, Pierre J., *Histoire des Institutions d'assurances en France* (Paris, 1956).

Riebesell, Paul, *Einführung in die Sachversicherungsmathematik* (Berlin: Mittler & Sohn, 1936)

Rodermund, Matthew, "Four Points of Confusion about Reinsurance: Comment", *The Journal of Risk and Insurance*, 32/1, (1965), 133-136.

Rohland, Eleonora, "From Wood to Stone: The Risk Management of Swiss Re in the Sundsvall Fire 1888", *Environment and History*, 17 (2011), 153-169.

Rohland, Eleonora, *Sharing the Risk. Fire, Climate and Disaster. Swiss Re, 1864-1906* (Lancashire: Carnegie Books, 2011).

Rossiyskiy Gosudarstvenny Istoricheskiy Arkiv (RGIA).

Rossi, Marie-Louise and Nicholas Lowe, "Regulating Reinsurance in the Global Market", *The Geneva Papers on Risk and Insurance*, 27, (2002), 122-133.

Rostow, Walt Whitman, "The Five Stages of Growth-A Summary", *The Stages of Economic Growth: A* Non-Communist Manifesto (Cambridge: Cambridge University Press, 1960), 4-16.

Rossiiskii gosudarstvennyi istoricheskii arkhiv (*RGIA*). [Russian State Historical, Archive]

San Román, Elena, "Las consecuencias pacíficas de la Gran Guerra: la movilización industrial", *Hispania*, 54 (1994), 611-58.

Schwepcke, Andreas (ed.), *Reinsurance: Principles and State of the Art* (Munich: Swiss RE Germany AG, 2004).

Shiu, Yung-Ming, "Reinsurance and Capital Structure: Evidence from the United Kingdom Non-Life Insurance Industry", *The Journal of Risk and Insurance*, 78/2, (2011).

Skipper Jr, Harold D., "Foreign insurers in emerging markets: Issues and concerns", *II F Occasional paper 1* (International Insurance Foundation, 1997).

Sigma 2, February (1977).

Straus, André, "Brève histoire de la réassurance avant 1945", *Risques* No. 37, (1999).

Sudriá, Carles, "Los beneficios de España durante la Gran Guerra. Una aproximación a la balanza de pagos española, 1914-1920", *Revista de Historia Económica*, 8 (1990), 363-96.

Sumitomo Marine & Fire Insurance Co. Ltd., *Sumitomo Marine & Fire Insurance, The First Century*, 1893-1993, (1993).

Swiss Re Corporate Archive.

Swiss Re, *A History of Insurance in Japan* (2013).

Sweden Re, *Annual reports* (1915-2013).

Taisei Fire and Marine Insurance Company Ltd., *The 40 Years History of Taisei Fire and Marine Insurance Company* (Japanese), (1991).

Taisei Fire and Marine Insurance Company Ltd., *A Brief History of Taisei Fire* (Japanese), (1970).

Taisho Marine and Fire Insurance Company Ltd., *The 40 Years History* (Japanese), (1961).

The Review

Titman, Sheridan and Wessels, Roberto, "The Determinants of Capital Structure Choice", *The Journal of Finance*, 43/1 (1988), 1-19.

Tokio Marine and Fire Insurance Company Ltd., *The Tokio Marine & Fire Insurance, 1879-1979, The First Century* (1980).

Tokio Marine and Fire Insurance Company Ltd., *The 80 Years History of Tokio Marine* (Japanese), (1964).

Tokio Marine and Fire Insurance Company Ltd., *The 60 Years History* (Japanese), (1940).

Tortella, Gabriel; Caruana de la Cagigas, Leonardo; García, José Luis, *MAPFRE from Mutual to Multinational* (Madrid: Mapfre, 2009).

Tortella, Gabriel; Caruana de la Cagigas, Leonardo; García Ruiz; José Luis; Manzano, Alberto y Pons Pons, Jerònia, *Historia del seguro en España* (Madrid: Fundación MAPFRE, 2014).

Thorin, Paul, *La réassurance contre l'incendie: son organisation technique et économique* (Orléans: Impr. Orleanaise, 1929).

United Nations, "Proceedings of the United Nations Conference on Trade and Development: First Session", 1, *Final Act and Report* (Geneva: United Nations, 1964).

United Nation, *Transnational Reinsurance Operations* (New York: United Nations Centre on Transnational Corporations, 1980).

Wehner, Christoph Julian, "Grenzen der Versicherbarkeit – Grenzen der Risikogesellschaft", *Archiv für Sozialgeschichte* 52 (2012), 581-605.

Yasuda Fire and Marine Insurance Company Ltd., *The Centenary History of Yasuda Fire* (Japanese), (1990).

Yasuda Fire and Marine Insurance Company Ltd., *The Yasuda Fire and Marine Insurance, 1888-1988, A Century of Achievement*, (1988).

Yasuda Fire and Marine Insurance Company Ltd., *The 80 Years History, Yasuda Fire and Marine Insurance* (Japanese), (1968).

Yoneyama, T., "The Great Kanto Earthquake and the Response of Insurance Companies: A Historical Lesson on the Impact of a Major Disaster", *Hitotsubashi Journal of Commerce and Management*, 43/1 (2009).

Yoneyama, T., "Japan: The Role of Insurance in the Rapid Modernization of Japan", in Borscheid, P. and Haueter, N. V. (eds.), *World Insurance: The Evolution of a Global Risk Network* (Oxford: Oxford University Press, 2012).

Wilkins, M., "Multinational enterprise in insurance: an historical overview", *Business History*, 51 (2009), 334-63.

"International Issues"

Studies in international relations, particularly historical, stem from the changing face of diplomacy over time, where the deeper forces at play, such as those once defined by Pierre Renouvin, are taken into account. Individual states, and those who define and implement their policies, are placed at the heart of global life. According to this concept, countries pursue a course of action by taking advantage of the most diverse range of tools they can rely on, such as economic or cultural resources, which act alone or interact with others.

The study of international relations grew into different fields of analysis during the twentieth century, but it is now subject to a new scrutiny in this era of globalisation. This concept, which coincides with the development of neo-liberal analysis since the 1980s, reveals a new awareness about the increased number of actors – NGOs and multinational companies, for example – but also the large autonomy they enjoy when it comes to action.

This series aims to portray these new perspectives and their impact on current research. Without casting aside studies in international relations that focus on states, it tries to better understand the diverse range of factors that play out on the world stage and how they relate to each other – from the high stakes in sport to the use of colonial memory. This series targets academics and analysts who wish to apply twentieth century history to contemporary thought.

Published Books

N° 1 – Catherine LANNEAU, *L'inconnue française. La France et les Belges francophones (1944-1945)*, 2008

N° 2 – Frédéric DESSBERG, *Le triangle impossible. Les relations franco-soviétiques et le facteur polonais dans les questions de sécurité en Europe (1924-1935)*, 2009

N° 3 – Agnès TACHIN, *Amie et rivale. La Grande-Bretagne dans l'imaginaire français à l'époque gaullienne*, 2009

N° 4 – Isabelle DAVION, *Mon voisin, cet ennemi. La politique de sécurité française face aux relations polono-tchécoslovaques entre 1919 et 1939*, 2009

N° 5 – Claire Laux, François-Joseph Ruggiu & Pierre Singaravélou (dir./eds.), *Au sommet de l'Empire. Les élites européennes dans les colonies (XVIe-XXe siècle) / At the Top of the Empire. European Elites in the Colonies (16th-20th Century)*, 2009

N° 6 – Frédéric Clavert, *Hjalmar Schacht, financier et diplomate (1930-1950)*, 2009

N° 7 – Robert Jablon, Laure Quennouëlle-Corre & André Straus, *Politique et finance à travers l'Europe du XXe siècle. Entretiens avec Robert Jablon*, 2009

N° 8 – Alain Beltran (ed.), *A Comparative History of National Oil Company*, 2010

N° 9 – Sarah Mohamed-Gaillard, *L'Archipel de la puissance ? La politique de la France dans le Pacifique Sud de 1946 à 1998*, 2010

N° 10 – Marie-Anne Matard-Bonucci, Anne Dulphy, Robert Frank & Pascal Ory (dir.), *Les relations culturelles internationales au vingtième siècle. De la diplomatie culturelle à l'acculturation*, 2010

N° 11 – Yves-Marie Péréon, *L'image de la France dans la presse américaine, 1936-1947*, 2011

N° 12 – Léonard Laborie, *L'Europe mise en réseaux. La France et la coopération internationale dans les postes et les télécommunications (années 1850-années 1950)*, 2010

N° 13 – Catherine Horel (dir.), *1908, la crise de Bosnie cent ans après*, 2011

N° 14 – Alain Beltran (ed.), *Oil Producing Countries and Oil Companies. From the Nineteenth Century to the Twenty-First Century*, 2011

N° 15 – Frédéric Dessberg & Éric Schnakenbourg (dir), *Les horizons de la politique extérieure française. Régions périphériques et espaces seconds dans la stratégie diplomatique et militaire de la France (XVIe-XXe siècles)*, 2011

N° 16 – Alya Aglan, Olivier Feiertag & Dzovinar Kévonian (dir.), *Humaniser le travail. Régimes économiques, régimes politiques et Organisations internationale du travail (1929-1969)*, 2011

N° 17 – Pierre Journoud & Cécile Menétrey-Monchau (dir./eds.), *Vietnam, 1968-1976. La sortie de guerre / Vietnam, 1968-1976. Exiting a War*, 2011

N° 18 – Louis Clerc, *La Finlande et l'Europe du Nord dans la diplomatie française. Relations bilatérales et intérêt national dans les considérations finlandaises et nordiques des diplomates et militaires français, 1917-1940*, 2011

N° 19 – Yann Decorzant, *La Société des Nations et la naissance d'une conception de la régulation économique internationale*, 2011

N° 20 – Lorenz Plassmann, *Comme dans une nuit de Pâques ? Les relations franco-grecques 1944-1981*, 2012

N° 21 – Alain Beltran (dir./ed.), *Le pétrole et la guerre / Oil and War*, 2012

N° 22 – Valentine Lomellini, Les relations dangereuses. *French Socialists, Communists and the Human Rights Issue in the Soviet Bloc*, 2012

N° 23 – Martial Libera, *Un rêve de puissance. La France et le contrôle de l'économie allemande (1942-1949)*, 2012

N° 24 – Séverine Antigone MARIN, *L'apprentissage de la mondialisation. Les milieux économiques allemands face à la réussite américaine (1876-1914)*, 2012

N° 25 – Claire SANDERSON & Mélanie TORRENT (dir./eds.), *La puissance britannique en question. Diplomatie et politique étrangère au 20e siècle/ Challenges to British Power Status. Foreign Policy and Diplomacy in the 20th Century*, 2012

N° 26 – Elena GRETCHANAIA, *« Je vous parlerai la langue de l'Europe... ». La francophonie en Russie (XVIIIe-XIXe siècles)*, 2012

N° 27 – Alfred WAHL, *Histoire de la Coupe du monde de football. Une mondialisation réussie*, 2013

N° 28 – Catherine FRAIXE, Lucia PICCIONI & Christophe POUPAULT (dir.), *Vers une Europe latine. Acteurs et enjeux des échanges culturels entre la France et l'Italie fasciste*, 2013

N° 29 – Danièle FRABOULET, Andrea M. LOCATELLI & Paolo TEDESCHI (eds.), *Historical and International Comparison of Business Interest Associations. 19th-20th Centuries*, 2013

N° 30 – Annie GUENARD-MAGET, *Une diplomatie culturelle dans les tensions internationales. La France en Europe centrale et orientale (1936-1940 / 1944-1951)*, 2014

N° 31 – Catherine HOREL (dir.), *Lès guerres balkaniques (1912-1913). Conflits, enjeux, mémoires*, 2014

N° 32 – Bruno DUMONS & Jean-Philippe WARREN (dir.), *Les zouaves pontificaux en France, en Belgique et au Québec. La mise en récit d'une expérience historique transnationale (XIXe-XXe siècles)*, 2015

N° 33 – Pierre CHABAL (dir.), *Concurrences interrégionales Europe-Asie au XXIe siècle*, 2015

N° 34 – Florent POUPONNEAU, *La politique française de non-prolifération nucléaire. De la division du travail diplomatique*, 2015

N° 35 – Alain BELTRAN (ed.), *Les routes du pétrole / Oil Routes*, 2016

N° 36 – Pierre CHABAL (dir.), *L'Organisation de coopération de Shanghai et la construction de la « nouvelle Asie »*, 2016

N° 37 – María Luisa AZPÍROZ, *Public Diplomacy. European and Latin American Perspectives*, 2015

N° 38 – Massimo BUCARELLI, Luca MICHELETTA, Luciano MONZALI & Luca RICCARDI (eds.), *Italy and Tito's Yugoslavia in the Age of International Détente*, 2016

N° 39 – Michel DUMOULIN & Catherine LANNEAU (dir.), *La biographie individuelle et collective dans le champ des relations internationales*, 2016

N° 40 – Sebastian SANTANDER, *Concurrences régionales dans un monde multipolaire émergent*, 2016

N° 41 – Alain BELTRAN, Éric BUSSIÈRE & Giuliano GARAVINI (dir.), *L'Europe et la question énergétique. Les années 1960/1980*, 2016